2:2-4

THE LAST DAYS SERIES

THE JEWS,
JERUSALEM & THE

COMING TEMPLE

DON STEWART

The Jews, Jerusalem, And The Coming Temple
Center Stage For The Final Countdown

Originally titled *The Jews, Jerusalem and the Next Temple*

By Don Stewart

English Versions Cited

The various English versions that we cite in this course, apart from the King James Version, all have copyrights. They are listed as follows.

TABLE OF CONTENTS

INTRODUCTION 5

CHAPTER 1: THE COMING TEMPLE: CENTER STAGE FOR THE FINAL
COUNTDOWN 9

PART ONE: THE PAST HISTORY OF JERUSALEM'S TEMPLE MOUNT 15

CHAPTER 2: THE LEGACY OF ABRAHAM: THE JEWS, JERUSALEM AND
MOUNT MORIAH 17

CHAPTER 3: THE ARK OF THE COVENANT: GOD'S SYMBOLIC PRESENCE
AMONG HIS PEOPLE 27

CHAPTER 4: SOLOMON'S MAGNIFICENT TEMPLE: A PERMANENT HOME IS
BUILT FOR THE ARK 35

CHAPTER 5: THE FIRST TEMPLE IS DESTROYED AS PREDICTED: THE PEOPLE
ARE SENT IN EXILE 41

CHAPTER 6: GOD'S PROMISES COME TRUE: THE JEWS RETURN FROM EXILE
AND A SECOND TEMPLE IS BUILT 51

CHAPTER 7: THE SECOND TEMPLE IS DEFILED BY INVADERS: THE TEMPLE
IS ENLARGED BY HEROD 61

CHAPTER 8: THE MESSIAH COMES AND IS REJECTED: JUDGMENT IS
PREDICTED UPON THE TEMPLE AND THE PEOPLE 69

CHAPTER 9: THE SECOND TEMPLE IS DESTROYED: ANOTHER JEWISH
EXILE BEGINS 81

CHAPTER 10: THE TEMPLE MOUNT IN RUIN: FUTILE ATTEMPTS ARE MADE
TO REBUILD 89

CHAPTER 11: THE TEMPLE MOUNT BECOMES IMPORTANT TO A NEW
RELIGION: ISLAM 103

CHAPTER 12: THE TEMPLE MOUNT CONTINUES TO BE DEFILED: THE JEWS
REMAIN IN FORCED EXILE 111

PART TWO: THE CURRENT STATE OF JERUSALEM AND THE TEMPLE MOUNT 121

CHAPTER 13: THE PREDICTED RESTORATION OF THE JEWS: THE TESTIMONY OF SCRIPTURE AND HISTORY 123

CHAPTER 14: 1948: GOD'S WORD IS FULFILLED AGAIN: THE MODERN STATE OF ISRAEL IS REBORN! 135

CHAPTER 15: 1967: SETTING THE STAGE FURTHER: JERUSALEM REUNITED UNDER ISRAELI RULE 145

CHAPTER 16: MODERN PREPARATIONS TO BUILD THE THIRD TEMPLE 159

CHAPTER 17: A MISSING PIECE OF THE TEMPLE PUZZLE: THE LOST ARK OF THE COVENANT 175

CHAPTER 18: TWO MAJOR OBSTACLES: WHERE AND HOW TO BUILD THE NEXT TEMPLE 185

PART THREE: THE COMING TEMPLE 203

CHAPTER 19: THE THIRD TEMPLE: THE ANTICIPATION OF SCRIPTURE AND ANCIENT BIBLE COMMENTATORS 205

CHAPTER 20: THE FALSE MESSIAH AND THE TEMPLE OF DOOM 223

CHAPTER 21: JESUS CHRIST RETURNS: THE END OF THE THIRD TEMPLE AND THE BEGINNING OF PEACE ON EARTH 239

CHAPTER 22: SUMMING IT ALL UP 247

APPENDIX 1: A SCIENTIFIC SEARCH FOR THE TEMPLE'S LOCATION (1983) 257

ABOUT THE AUTHOR 269

Introduction

Why are the Jewish people miraculously back in their own land after a two-thousand-year absence? Why does the city of Jerusalem remain the focus of international attention? Why are certain Jews now planning to build another Temple on Jerusalem's Temple Mount? Will another Temple be built? Will this coming Temple bring peace on earth as the Jews hope? Is it possible the lost Ark of the Covenant will be found and placed in this future Temple? Why is this one city, Jerusalem, and this one piece of real estate, the Temple Mount, so important to Jews, Muslims, and Christians?

The Bible has much to say on these and other matters pertaining to the Jews, Jerusalem, and the coming Temple. Jerusalem's Temple Mount has already been the scene of many important biblical events. According to the way many Christians understand Bible prophecy, the Temple Mount will be center-stage, ground zero, for coming events that will signal the return of Jesus Christ to the earth. Therefore, the study of this subject is of immense importance.

THE AMAZING JEWS

The Jews are the most remarkable nation on the earth. Their history testifies to the miraculous power and faithfulness of God. As the Bible has clearly predicted, and against all odds of history, the Jews have returned to their ancient homeland after two thousand years of wandering the globe. This return has set the stage for end-time Bible prophecies to be fulfilled.

JERUSALEM—THE CITY OF PEACE

For all intents and purposes, the city of Jerusalem should be like any other city. Jerusalem has no natural wealth, no oil reserves, and no great strategic value. Yet it is at the center of today's headlines and it is the focal point of debate among the great powers of the world. No other city in the world has been as desired, and fought over, as Jerusalem—the city of peace. In its history it has been attacked by armies of the Babylonians, Persians, Greeks, Ptolemies, Seleucids, Romans, Byzantines, Arabs, Seljuks, Crusaders, Mongols, Mamelukes, Turks, British and Jordanians. Even with all of this, Jerusalem remains a sacred symbol to three great religions: Judaism, Christianity, and Islam.

The Bible clearly spells out the reason for Jerusalem's importance—it is center stage in the eternal plan of God.

THE COMING TEMPLE

Finally, we come to Jerusalem's Temple Mount—the place where the First and Second Temple of the Jews formerly stood. According to a literal understanding of Bible prophecy, a Third Temple is going to be built before Jesus Christ returns. This future Temple will be the site where many important end-time events will occur. Therefore, it is crucial that we understand what the Scripture says about these issues.

We are fortunate to be living in these times. For the last two thousand years, careful Bible students have been looking for, and have been expecting, certain prophesied events to take place. Our generation has witnessed the fulfillment of many of these long-awaited predictions. Therefore, as we consider the subject of the Jews, Jerusalem, and the coming Temple, the words of Jesus are most appropriate.

> But when these things begin to take place, stand up and lift up your heads, because your redemption is near (Luke 21:28 HCSB).

A MODERN ATTEMPT TO REBUILD THE TEMPLE

On July 28, 2014, The Temple Institute, an organization in Jerusalem which works toward the rebuilding of the Third Temple, began a revolutionary campaign to literally rebuild it—through the power of crowdfunding. Headlines under the title "Don't make history. Make the future. Build the Third Temple." Among other things, their online ad read as follows . . .

> Now is time for one of its most ambitious projects yet: completing architectural plans for the actual construction, fusing ancient texts and modern technology. While strictly adhering to the religious requirements set forth in Biblical texts, the Third Temple will also be equipped with every modern amenity: full computerization, underground parking, temperature control, elevators, docks for public transportation, wheelchair access, and much more.

What is clear from the Bible that Israel is God's clock. The nation is the hour hand, the city of Jerusalem the minute hand, and the Temple Mount the second hand.

So as we keep our eyes on the country, the city, and the Temple Mount let us now turn to the Bible, as well as to the historical record, to discover the amazing adventure of the Jews, Jerusalem and the Coming Temple.

CHAPTER 1

The Coming Temple:
Center Stage for the Final Countdown

The temple in Jerusalem will be yet rebuilt by the Jews in unbelief, and be the scene of wickedness greater than has ever appeared . . . While, then, the temple had been destroyed at the date of the writing of Revelation [approximately A.D. 90], it was hereby predicted that it would be rebuilt . . . Till the Jew is brought back to his own land, and the temple and sacrifices restored, the prophetic part of the Apocalypse does not begin.

Robert Govett, 1861[1]

We are living in exciting times! Since the ascension of Jesus Christ into heaven, Christians have been looking forward to the day when certain biblical prophecies will be fulfilled which will eventually culminate in His return to the earth.

In fact, Jesus predicted the Jews would be scattered from their land, have their Temple destroyed, and that their holy city of Jerusalem would fall under the domination of other nations. Luke records Him saying the following.

They will fall by the edge of the sword and be led away as captives among all nations. Jerusalem will be trampled down

1. Robert Govett, *Govett on Revelation*, Volume I, Miami Springs, Florida, 1981, reprint of originally published in London in 1861 titled *The Apocalypse: Expounded by Scripture*. p. 497

by the Gentiles until the times of the Gentiles are fulfilled (Luke 21:24 NET).

All of this has literally occurred just as He predicted.

Before Christ returns, the Bible foresees the Jews coming back to their land in unbelief of Jesus as Messiah, gaining control over Jerusalem, and also building a new Temple.

THE FULFILLMENT BEGINS

Our generation has witnessed the return of the Jews to their land, and the rebirth of the state of Israel. We have also seen Jerusalem unified by the Israelis. We are now witnessing the preparations being made for the construction of a new Temple.

WE ARE NOT SURPRISED TO SEE THIS OCCURRING

To see these events begin to unfold in our day and age is not surprising. Indeed, they have been predicted by Scripture, and also by those who have interpreted the Bible literally. As we shall see, the return of the Jews, and the building of a Third Temple, has been predicted for the last two thousand years by many Christians who interpret Bible prophecy in a literal manner. They believed God's promises by faith.

Today we do not have to look forward to these promises merely by faith. In fact, they are beginning to happen right in front of our very eyes!

THE RETURN HAS BEEN FORETOLD

The idea that the Jews will be restored to their land has been taught by the Christian church ever since the Jews were removed from their land in A.D. 70. Writing in 1875, after the Jews had been already scattered for 1,800 years, John R. Caldwell noted.

> In many Scriptures the present scattered condition of the nation Israel is foretold, and in connection therewith, there

is also foretold their being gathered again into their own land. Some have tried to attach only a spiritual significance to those Scriptures which speak of Israel's restoration, whilst forced to admit that they are literally, and not figuratively, scattered. But this cannot be tenable in the face of . . . Scripture.[2]

William Blackstone wrote in 1880.

But perhaps you say: "I don't believe the Israelites are to be restored to Canaan, and Jerusalem rebuilt." Dear reader have you read the declarations of God's word about it? Surely nothing is more plainly stated in Scripture.[3]

One early 20th century writer put it this way.

There is nothing more certain from the word of God than that the Jews, who are now dispersed throughout the world, will be restored to their own land for "He that scattereth Israel will gather him" (Jeremiah 31:10).[4]

THE JEWS WILL RETURN TO THEIR LAND IN UNBELIEF

The Bible predicts a final gathering of the Jews to their ancient homeland. However, Scripture says that they will return to the land in unbelief of Jesus as their Messiah. This has been noted by Bible students of the past.

For example, the great scholar of the nineteenth century, Bishop B.W. Newton, concluded the following after his study of Scripture.

I observed . . . the history of Israel during the time of their punishment and subjection to the gentiles, is distributed into three

---

2. John R. Caldwell, *Things To Come*, London, James E. Hawkins, 1875, p. 24

3. William Blackstone, *Jesus Is Coming*, Old Tappan New Jersey, Fleming Revell, 1932, p. 162

4. Edward Dennett, *The Blessed Hope*, London, G. Morrish, 1910, p. 48

distinct divisions: the first extending from Nebuchadnezzar to their dispersion by the Romans—the second being the present period of their dispersion—the third, the yet future period of their national reestablishment in unbelief. . . . We are in the interval, the period of dispersion, now. It will terminate when Jerusalem is nationally reconstituted.[5]

That future period, that Newton and others spoke of, is no longer future. The Jews have returned, in unbelief, to their Promised Land after an absence of almost 1,900 years.

THEY WILL BUILD THE THIRD TEMPLE

Two parts of this "last days" prophecy have been literally fulfilled. Another part is still future and this will be the main concern of this book—the construction of a future Temple along with the renewal of the ancient sacrificial system.

When asked for a specific sign concerning His Second Coming, Jesus gave His disciples a sign that has to do with the Temple in Jerusalem. According to Jesus, a specific event that takes place in the Temple will be the incident that begins a three and one half year period of God's judgment upon the earth. This awful period is known as the "great tribulation." At the end of this three-and-a-half-year period of great tribulation, Christ will then return to the earth.

However, before these events can transpire, the Temple must be built and functioning. This fact has kept Bible students closely monitoring any movement toward the building of the next Temple.

THERE ARE ANCIENT PREDICTIONS THAT THIS WILL OCCUR

The prediction of the Temple's rebuilding is something that has been taught by Christians for the last two thousand years. For example,

---

5. B.W. Newton, *How B.W. Newton Learned Prophetic Truth*, London, Sovereign Grace Advent Testimony, 1880, p. 4

Irenaeus, living in the second century A.D. wrote concerning the predicted Antichrist who will come to this rebuilt Temple.

> He will reign a time, times, and half a time (Daniel 7:25) (i.e. three and a half years) and will sit in the temple at Jerusalem; then the Lord shall come from heaven and cast him into the lake of fire, and shall bring to the saints the time of reigning, the seventh day of hallowed rest, and give to Abraham the promised inheritance.[6]

In 1881, Walter Scott asked and answered the question about the coming Temple.

> Will the temple be rebuilt and a Jewish ritual established? Yes. The Antichrist to come will make the Temple the seat of his worship (2 Thess. ii. 4). It is also regarded as existing with its daily sacrifice and worship, during the course of the future judgments (Rev. xi.; Isa. lxvi. 6; Dan xii 11). The Lord too, in His great prophetic discourse (Matt. xxiv. 15), pointed to that "holy place" as yet future even then. Scripture records nothing as to the erection of it, but simply notes the fact. The prophetic portions of Daniel also suppose the existence of a Temple, and consequently a Jewish ritual as of old.[7]

The evidence is clear: The Temple will be rebuilt!

SUMMARY TO CHAPTER 1

Today we are witnessing the fulfillment of predictions that were made thousands of years ago. In unbelief of Jesus, the Jews have returned to their land after a two-thousand-year absence, Jerusalem is once again under their control, and preparations are being made to build a new Temple. Bible prophecy is in the process of being fulfilled.

---

6. Irenaeus, *Against Heresies*, Book V, Chapter 30, Paragraph 4

7. Walter Scott, *Future Events*, Oak Park, Ill., Bible Truth Press, originally published 1881, 1977 reprint, pp. 48, 49

It is with this backdrop in mind that we consider the story of the Jews, Jerusalem, and their holy Temple—from the time of the building of the First Temple, to the Second Coming of Jesus Christ, and the setting up of His Temple and His Kingdom.

PART 1

The Past History Of
Jerusalem's Temple Mount

It is difficult to overestimate the importance of Jerusalem's Temple Mount. Three of the world's great religions, Judaism, Christianity, and Islam hold it in the highest regard. To Judaism and Islam, the Temple Mount is the holiest site among a city of many "holy sites."

How did Jerusalem and the Temple Mount come to be so important? Why do all three of these religions believe that the Temple Mount will be the spot where great events will someday take place?

In our first section, we will consider the history of the Temple Mount, from its earliest biblical reference until modern times. In doing so, we will discover why this one plot of ground is of so much importance to these three world religions, as well as to the future of our planet.

CHAPTER 2

The Legacy of Abraham:
The Jews, Jerusalem and Mount Moriah

There is an outcropping of starkly bare rough limestone rock in Jerusalem which for thirty centuries past has gripped the minds and hearts of the sons of men as being the most sacred spot on earth. Known to the Jews as the Temple Mount and to the Muslims as the Noble Sanctuary. Tradition and legend blend together where it is difficult to separate the two . . . Few places in the world have been . . . as sacred as this city, this flattened mountain and this rock. While the world lasts and as long as the sons of men believe that one spot on it is more sacred and hallowed than another, this will remain so.[1]

Solomon Steckoll

In every age, the memory of Jerusalem has stirred the deepest feelings. Jews, Christians, and Mohammedans turn to it with reverent affection. It almost seems as if in some sense each could call it his 'happy home,' the 'name ever dear' to him. For our holiest thoughts of the past, and our happiest hopes for the future, connect themselves with 'the city of our God.'[2]

Alfred Edersheim

1. Solomon Steckoll, *The Temple Mount*, London, Tom Stacey Publishers, 1972, p. 9
2. Alfred Edersheim, *The Temple*, Grand Rapids, Eerdmans, reprinted 1992, p. 23

The story of Jerusalem, the Jews, and the Temple Mount takes us back some forty centuries—to the time of Abraham.

In the first eleven chapters of the book of Genesis we have the record of God creating the universe, creating humankind, the Fall of humankind, the Flood of Noah, and the Tower of Babel.

Beginning at the twelfth chapter of Genesis, and continuing through the rest of Scripture, we have the story of God's dealings with humankind through a specific race—the descendants of Abraham.

ABRAHAM'S IMPORTANCE TO THE WORLD

The importance of Abram (whose name was later changed to Abraham) cannot be overestimated. Today there are three major religions (Judaism, Christianity, and Islam) that believe in only one God. Each of these world religions has one central person whom they revere.

The outstanding figure among the Jews is Moses, the giver of the Law. The Muslims look to Muhammad, the last and greatest of the prophets. Christians worship Jesus, God's only Son, and the promised Messiah.

Yet each of these three world religions trace their beginnings back some forty centuries ago to the same man, Abraham. Jesus, Moses, and Muhammad were all physical descendants of this man Abraham.

Therefore, Abraham is a central figure in three of the major world religions in our day.

THE CALL OF ABRAM

The reason for Abraham's importance is because of a specific covenant, or agreement, that God made with him. Four thousand years ago, God called Abraham out of a sinful culture, and made him promises that still apply today. We read the following in Genesis.

> The LORD had said to Abram, "Go from your country, your people and your father's household to the land I will show

you. "I will make you into a great nation, and I will bless you; I will make your name great, and you will be a blessing. I will bless those who bless you, and whoever curses you I will curse; and all peoples on earth will be blessed through you" (Genesis 12:1-3 NIV).

God took this one man from the place where his fathers had served other gods and led him to the Promised Land. According to God's promise, this land would belong to his descendants forever.

THE PROMISE OF DESCENDANTS

Among other things, God promised Abraham that he would have a tremendous number of descendants. The Bible says Abraham believed God's promise.

> He took him outside and said, "Look up at the sky and count the stars—if indeed you can count them." Then he said to him, "So shall your offspring be." Abram believed the Lord, and he credited it to him as righteousness (Genesis 15:5,6 NIV).

The Lord, the living God, made Abraham a promise of many descendants and he believed the promise.

THE BORDERS OF THE LAND ARE DEFINED

In addition, God specifically laid out to Abraham the borders of the land that was to belong to him and his descendants. The Bible puts it this way.

> The LORD said to Abram after Lot had parted from him, "Look around from where you are, to the north and south, to the east and west. All the land that you see I will give to you and your offspring forever. I will make your offspring like the dust of the earth, so that if anyone could count

the dust, then your offspring could be counted. Go, walk through the length and breadth of the land, for I am giving it to you" (Genesis 13:14-17 NIV).

The Lord also said.

On that day the LORD made a covenant with Abram and said, "To your descendants I give this land, from the Wadi of Egypt to the great river, the Euphrates, the land of the Kenites, Kenizzites, Kadmonites, Hittites, Perizzites, Rephaites, Amorites, Canaanites, Girgashites and Jebusites" (Genesis 15:18,19 NIV).

Such were to be the borders of the Promised Land.

THE PROMISES TO ABRAHAM ARE REPEATED

In Genesis 17, these promises were repeated and enlarged upon. In addition, we are told that the promises made to Abraham and his descendants are everlasting. God said.

I will establish my covenant as an everlasting covenant between me and you and your descendants after you for the generations to come, to be your God and the God of your descendants after you. The whole land of Canaan, where you now reside as a foreigner, I will give as an everlasting possession to you and your descendants after you; and I will be their God (Genesis 17:7,8 NIV).

This covenant, or agreement, that God made with Abraham's descendants *cannot* be revoked. In fact, it was later confirmed to Abraham with an oath.

The Book of Genesis has the following to say about what occurred between the Lord and Abraham. We read.

The angel of the LORD called to Abraham from heaven a second time and said, "I swear by myself, declares the LORD, that because you have done this and have not withheld your son, your only son, I will surely bless you and make your descendants as numerous as the stars in the sky and as the sand on the seashore. Your descendants will take possession of the cities of their enemies, and through your offspring all nations on earth will be blessed, because you have obeyed me" (Genesis 22:15-18 NIV).

God re-confirmed the covenant with Abraham.

GOD'S PROMISES TO ABRAHAM ARE MANY

The Lord made a number of promises to Abraham and his descendants. We can sum them up in the following way.

1. A great nation will descend from Abraham and his wife Sarah.

2. Abraham's name shall be blessed.

3. Whoever blesses Abraham's descendants will be blessed.

4. Whoever curses Abraham's descendants will be cursed.

5. His descendants will continue forever.

6. His descendants will inherit a Promised Land with clearly defined borders.

7. The ownership of the land belongs to them forever.

Against seemingly impossible odds, these promises have been literally fulfilled. The fact that they have been fulfilled, as the Lord had promised, demonstrates both God's existence and faithfulness.

THE PROMISED SON

One special promise that God made to Abraham was that of a son. Abraham and his wife Sarah waited year after year for the promise to be fulfilled. Yet no child was born. Eventually they reached the place where they were beyond the child-bearing years. In a lapse of faith, Abraham took his handmaiden Hagar and had a son through her. The son's name was Ishmael. The Bible says Abraham and Sarah wished Ishmael to be the son of promise. We read.

> So she said to Abram, "The LORD has kept me from having children. Go, sleep with my slave; perhaps I can build a family through her." Abram agreed to what Sarai said . . . He slept with Hagar, and she conceived. When she knew she was pregnant, she began to despise her mistress. So Hagar bore Abram a son, and Abram gave the name Ishmael to the son she had borne (Genesis 16:2,4,15 NIV).

Ishmael became the father of the Arab people. While Abraham and Sarah wanted God's promises to be fulfilled in Ishmael, he was *not* the son that God had promised.

THE LORD APPEARS TO ABRAHAM

The Bible says that the Lord appeared to Abraham when he and his wife Sarah were advanced in age. Sending three angels, or messengers, to Abraham, the Lord promised that a son would be born to them the next year. Sarah laughed when she overheard the promise. The Bible explains it this way.

> The LORD appeared to Abraham near the great trees of Mamre while he was sitting at the entrance to his tent in the heat of the day . . . Then one [of the three messengers] said, "I will surely return to you about this time next year, and Sarah your wife will have a son." Now Sarah was listening at the entrance to the tent, which was behind him. Abraham and Sarah were already very old, and Sarah was past the age of childbearing. So Sarah laughed to herself as she thought, "After I am worn out and my lord is old, will I now have

this pleasure?" Then the LORD said to Abraham, "Why did Sarah laugh and say, 'Will I really have a child, now that I am old?' Is anything too hard for the LORD? I will return to you at the appointed time next year, and Sarah will have a son" (Genesis 18:1,10-14 NIV).

Though both Abraham and his wife Sarah were beyond the child-bearing years, God proved to be faithful to His Word. Abraham and Sarah had a son whom they named Isaac, which means "laughter."

ABRAHAM IS BROUGHT TO MOUNT MORIAH

About thirty years later, when Isaac had grown into a man, God asked Abraham to make the supreme sacrifice. After waiting so long for a son to be born, the Bible records that God told Abraham to take this beloved son of promise and offer him as a burnt offering.

Some time later God tested Abraham. He said to him, "Abraham!" "Here I am," he replied. Then God said, "Take your son, your only son, whom you love—Isaac—and go to the region of Moriah. Sacrifice him there as a burnt offering on a mountain I will show you" (Genesis 22:1-2 NIV).

Abraham acted in obedience to God, and went on a three-day journey to the site which God had chosen—the land of Moriah. The site that God brought Abraham, Mt. Moriah, would later become the city of Jerusalem.

THE BINDING OF ISAAC

When they reached the specific mountain that God had chosen, Abraham was prepared to sacrifice his only son Isaac.

Isaac said to his father Abraham, "My father?" "What is it, my son?" he replied. "Here is the fire and the wood," Isaac said, "but where is the lamb for the burnt offering?" "God will provide for himself the lamb for the burnt offering, my son," Abraham replied. The two of them continued on together (Genesis 22:7-8 NET).

At the last moment, God stopped the hand of Abraham as he was about to sacrifice his son. Instead, Abraham offered a ram as a sacrifice on Mt. Moriah in place of his son. There Abraham appropriately named the spot.

> So Abraham called that place The LORD Will Provide. And to this day it is said, "On the mountain of the LORD it will be provided" (Genesis 22:14 NIV).

Abraham looked forward to the day when God would provide another sacrifice at that location.

IS THIS THE TEMPLE SITE?

Since God guided Abraham to a specific spot, the Jews see this as prophetic. They commonly believe that this was the exact site where the Temple was later built. It is also an ancient Jewish tradition that many other significant events occurred of this exact spot. Rabbi Chaim Richman writes.

> The exact location of the altar is extremely precise, and can never be changed . . . and it is a universally accepted tradition that the place on which David and Solomon built the altar (on the site of the threshing floor of Aravnah) is the very same spot on which Abraham built the altar on which he bound Isaac . . . this is the same spot on which Noah built an altar upon leaving the ark, and this is the altar which Cain and Abel offered their sacrifices, and upon which Adam was created. The sages said: 'Adam was created from the very spot that atones for him.'[3]

---

3. Chaim Richman, *The Odyssey Of The Third Temple*, Israel Publications And Productions, n.d., p. 12

Among many Jews, therefore, it is believed that this spot on Mount Moriah was where Adam was created, where Cain and Abel built their altar, where Noah built his altar after the Flood, as well as the site of the Temple. There is, however, no biblical evidence for any of these events occurring at this place—apart from Abraham's binding of Isaac.

THE FUTURE SITE OF THE TEMPLE

The Jews also believe that this exact spot will be the site where their future Temple will be built. Chaim Richman also wrote.

> The hill on which Adam offered his first sacrifice after he was created thereon, where Noah built his altar and sacrificed, when he left the Ark, where Abraham erected his altar to bring the supreme sacrifice—his son Isaac; on this hill Solomon built the first Temple, there also the second one stood and in this very place the Third Temple will be erected.[4]

IT MAY BE GOLGOTHA, NOT THE TEMPLE SITE

Some Christians believe that the spot to which Abraham was directed was not the eventual site of the Temple, but rather the site of Golgotha (Calvary)—the place of Jesus' crucifixion. Indeed, the two traditional sites for Golgotha are found on Mount Moriah. There are some facts that may indicate that Abraham took Isaac to Golgotha rather than the present-day Temple Mount.

First, Golgotha is on higher ground than the Temple Mount. Second, during the time of Abraham, there was an existing Jebusite city on the southern slope of the Temple Mount. Many Bible students believe it unlikely that Abraham would have taken Isaac to sacrifice him directly above that pagan city. However, the exact place of the binding of Isaac cannot be precisely determined.

---

4. Richman, p. 14

Whether we are dealing with the same location, or two different locations on Mount Moriah, one thing is clear: The Jews will build the future Temple on the Temple Mount in the city of Jerusalem.

SUMMARY TO CHAPTER 2

Through Abraham and his descendants God promised to fulfill His Divine plan. Indeed, Abraham and his offspring would testify to the faithfulness of God and His promises. The entire world would know that God was providentially watching over them. The Bible says that the nation of Israel began in a supernatural way. Isaac, the son of promise, was miraculously born to Abraham and Sarah, after they had passed the childbearing years.

When Isaac had grown to be a man, Abraham was ordered to sacrifice him at a specific spot that God determined. Abraham obeyed, and God brought him to the appointed spot to sacrifice Isaac—Mt. Moriah— the same mountain range where Jerusalem would later be built, and the Temple constructed. As Abraham was about to offer his son, the Lord stopped him. God then promised to provide another sacrifice on that mountain in the future.

Indeed, the stage was now set for the promises of God to be fulfilled toward Abraham's descendants, the city of Jerusalem, and that specific mountain where God instructed Abraham to sacrifice Isaac.

CHAPTER 3

The Ark of the Covenant:
God's Symbolic Presence Among His People

Have them make an ark of acacia wood.

(Exodus 25:10)

As God had promised, a great nation sprung from Abraham through his son Isaac. According to God's Word, Abraham's descendants, Israel, would inherit a land where they would live as His special people as well as be a witness of Him to the world. There was, however, a warning contained with the promises. The Lord warned Abraham that before they entered the Promised Land, his descendants would have to live as slaves in a foreign land for 400 years.

Scripture says the following.

> Then the Lord said to Abram, "Know for certain that your descendants will be strangers in a foreign country. They will be enslaved and oppressed for four hundred years. But I will execute judgment on the nation that they will serve. Afterward they will come out with many possessions. But as for you, you will go to your ancestors in peace and be buried at a good old age. In the fourth generation your descendants will return here, for the sin of the Amorites has not yet reached its limit" (Genesis 15:13-15 NET).

All of this was literally fulfilled. After 400 years of living as slaves in the land of Egypt, God sent them a deliverer named Moses. Under Moses' leadership, and the miraculous power of God, the people were brought out of Egyptian bondage. The children of Israel came out of Egypt with much gold and silver as God had told Abraham they would. The Lord then sent them on their way to the Promised Land.

THE TEN COMMANDMENTS ARE GIVEN

On their journey to the Land of Promise, the people stopped at Mt. Sinai. Moses went alone to the top of the mountain to commune with God. Forty days later, Moses came down from the mountain with two tablets of stone containing the Ten Commandments—written by the hand of God.

The people, however, had grown impatient with Moses' stay on the Mount. They constructed a golden calf, and worshipped it as the sacred object that delivered them from Egypt. When Moses came down from the mountain, and saw what had happened, he threw down the two tablets breaking them into pieces.

After judgment was handed out upon those responsible for this idolatry, Moses returned to the mountain, and a second set of tablets was made by God's hand.

THE MOST SACRED OBJECT EVER BUILT: THE ARK OF THE COVENANT

God then instructed Moses to construct a sacred object, which would not only contain the Ten Commandments, but would symbolize His presence among the people. This holy object was the Ark of the Covenant.

The command to build the Ark of the Covenant is recorded in the Book of Exodus. The Lord told Moses to do the following.

> They are to make an ark of acacia wood—its length is to be three feet nine inches, its width two feet three inches, and its height two feet three inches. You are to overlay it with pure

gold-both inside and outside you must overlay it, and you are to make a surrounding border of gold over it. You are to cast four gold rings for it and put them on its four feet, with two rings on one side and two rings on the other side. You are to make poles of acacia wood, overlay them with gold, and put the poles into the rings at the sides of the ark in order to carry the ark with them. The poles must remain in the rings of the ark; they must not be removed from it. You are to put into the ark the testimony that I will give to you (Exodus 25:10-16 NET).

The Ark of the Covenant, was a rectangular container, or chest, made out of acacia wood and lined inside and outside with pure gold. The Hebrew word translated "Ark" means "box" or "chest." In fact, the word is used elsewhere in the Old Testament of a "chest." We read.

Jehoiada the priest took a chest and bored a hole in its lid. He placed it beside the altar, put into the chest all the money that was brought to the temple of the LORD. Whenever they saw that there was a large amount of money in the chest, the royal secretary and the high priest came, counted the money that had been brought into the temple of the LORD and put it into bags (2 Kings 12:9-10 NIV).

This suggests that the primary function of the Ark was to be a container. The object was called the Ark of God because it was the only visible representation of the throne of God on the earth. In the Book of First Samuel we read the following.

The lamp of God had not yet gone out, and Samuel was lying down in the house of the LORD, where the ark of God was (1 Samuel 3:3 NIV).

The ark of God represented His presence.

ON TOP OF THE ARK WAS THE MERCY SEAT, THE ATONEMENT COVER

All around the top of the Ark was a gold rectangular plate known as the "Mercy Seat" or "Atonement Cover." It was to be placed on top of the Ark, having the exact same dimensions. The Lord told Moses to make it as follows.

> You are to make an atonement lid of pure gold; its length is to be three feet nine inches, and its width is to be two feet three inches . . . You are to put the atonement lid on top of the ark, and in the ark you are to put the testimony I am giving you (Exodus 25:17,21 NET).

The translation "Mercy Seat" has led to misconceptions. The basic meaning of the Hebrew word, which is translated Mercy Seat is, "to cover." The Mercy Seat was the *cover* or the *lid* of the Ark. However, the Mercy Seat was more than a simple covering, it was an "atonement covering"—the place where sins were covered up.

Therefore, the term has been various translated as the "Mercy Seat," "atonement cover," "atonement lid" or "propitiatory lid."

God promised that He would speak to His people from above this sacred object. We read His promise.

> There, above the cover between the two cherubim that are over the ark of the covenant law, I will meet with you and give you all my commands for the Israelites (Exodus 25:22 NIV).

It was from this particular place where the living God spoke to His people.

THERE WERE TWO CHERUBIM ON THE ATONEMENT COVER (THE MERCY SEAT)

Facing each other at opposite ends of the Atonement Cover, or the Mercy Seat, stood two cherubim made out of hammered gold.

Cherubim are winged creatures that represent heavenly beings in God's service. The cherubim covered this sacred object with their spread out wings. The Bible says.

> And make two cherubim out of hammered gold at the ends of the cover. Make one cherub on one end and the second cherub on the other; make the cherubim of one piece with the cover, at the two ends. The cherubim are to have their wings spread upward, overshadowing the cover with them. The cherubim are to face each other, looking toward the cover (Exodus 25:18-20 NIV).

THE CHERUBIM ON THE ARK COMPARED TO THE CHERUBIM IN EDEN

There is an important observation that we should make between the cherubim placed upon the top of the Ark of the Covenant and those stationed in Eden after Adam and Eve sinned.

In Eden, the cherubim were placed in such a way as to keep people out of the Garden. In other words, they were facing outward from Eden. The Bible explains it this way.

> So the Lord God banished him from the Garden of Eden to work the ground from which he had been taken. After he drove the man out, he placed on the east side of the Garden of Eden cherubim and a flaming sword flashing back and forth to guard the way to the tree of life (Genesis 3:23-24 NIV).

In contrast, the cherubim on top of the Ark were not facing outward but rather inward toward the presence of the Lord. Consequently, instead of turning people away from God, these cherubim represented the place where humans could meet God, through an intermediary, the High Priest.

While Adam's sin caused humanity to be exiled from the presence of the Lord, the Ark, stationed in the Holy of Holies in the Tabernacle, allowed humans to once again enter into His Holy presence by means of a representative from the human race. This is a wonderful picture! Indeed, it demonstrates that the Lord had made a way for the human race to once again to have access to Him.

THE CONTENTS OF THE ARK

The Lord gave specific orders as to what the Ark would contain. The Ten Commandments, written by the hand of God, were placed inside the Ark. Later in Israel's history, Moses recounted the story.

> Then I came back down the mountain and put the tablets in the ark I had made, as the LORD commanded me, and they are there now (Deuteronomy 10:5 NIV).

The Bible says the Ark also contained Aaron's rod that budded, and a pot of manna.

> And after the second curtain there was a tent called the holy of holies. It contained the golden altar of incense and the ark of the covenant covered entirely with gold. In this ark were the golden urn containing the manna, Aaron's rod that budded, and the stone tablets of the covenant (Hebrews 9:3-4 NET).

This is the biblical description of the contents of the ark.

THE PLACE OF MEETING: THE TABERNACLE

After the directions were given for building the Ark, Moses was ordered to build a portable sanctuary which would house the sacred object. This temporary structure was the "Tabernacle." The Lord gave Moses the commandment to build this place of meeting.

> Then have them make a sanctuary for me, and I will dwell among them (Exodus 25:8 NIV).

God's visible presence would be among His people.

IT WAS A LARGE TENT

The Tabernacle was a huge tent about 45 feet long. It was divided into two rooms. The outer room of the Tabernacle, called the "Holy Place," was about 30 feet by 15 feet in size.

The inner room, the Holy of Holies, measured about 15 by 15 feet in size. A richly decorated veil divided the two rooms. In the Holy of Holies, there stood only the Ark of the Covenant.

IT WAS A TEMPORARY PLACE FOR THE GLORY OF GOD

The Tabernacle was the temporary resting place for God's glory. Its duty was to house the Ark. Because of its importance, God instructed Moses to build the Ark before anything else, including the Tabernacle itself.

SPECIAL WISDOM WAS GIVEN TO THE BUILDERS

The Ark was built upon Moses' order. To complete their task, the builders were given special wisdom from the Lord. God said to Moses.

> Moreover, I have appointed Oholiab son of Ahisamak, of the tribe of Dan, to help him. Also I have given ability to all the skilled workers to make everything I have commanded you: the tent of meeting, the ark of the covenant law with the atonement cover on it, and all the other furnishings of the tent (Exodus 31:6-7 NIV).

In this case, the builders were given special wisdom and skill.

THE WORK WAS FINISHED

The Bible records that the work was finished as ordered. It was at the beginning of the second year of the Exodus from Egypt that the Ark of the Covenant was brought to Moses.

> So all the work on the tabernacle, the tent of meeting, was completed. The Israelites did everything just as the LORD commanded Moses. Then they brought the tabernacle to

Moses: the tent and all its furnishings, its clasps, frames, crossbars, posts and bases; the covering of ram skins dyed red and the covering of another durable leather and the shielding curtain; the ark of the covenant law with its poles and the atonement cover (Exodus 39:32-35 NIV).

The Ten Commandments were then placed inside the Ark of the Covenant, and the Atonement Cover was secured on top. The children of Israel then continued their march to the Promised Land.

The Tabernacle was moved each day as the children of Israel marched in the wilderness. Every day they moved, the Tabernacle was dismantled and carried on poles. At night, the tribes were encamped in a square formation, with the Holy Ark of the Covenant at the center.

In fact, this placing of the Ark at the center of the camp was symbolic of an important biblical truth: everything on earth, as in heaven, centers around the God of the Bible!

SUMMARY TO CHAPTER 3

The Ark of the Covenant was the most sacred object God has ever ordered humanity to construct. Not only did it contain the tablets of the Law—the Ten Commandments that were written with the hand of God—it symbolized the covenant, the promises that God has made with His people.

The Tabernacle was ordered built for a purpose—to house the Ark. The Tabernacle was only a temporary home for this sacred object before a more permanent structure could be built.

Once in the Promised Land, God would eventually direct them to the exact site which He had chosen to build a lasting home for the Ark.

In fact, that precise site will be center-stage, ground zero, for momentous events which are still to take place in the future. Indeed, these events will lead to the Second Coming of Jesus Christ to the earth!

CHAPTER 4

Solomon's Magnificent Temple: A Permanent Home Is Built for the Ark

But will God really dwell on earth? The heavens, even the highest heaven, cannot contain you. How much less this temple I have built! (1 Kings 8:27)

King Solomon

After forty years of wandering in the wilderness, the children of Israel entered the land that God promised to the descendants of Abraham.

ISRAEL BEGINS TO CONQUER

Once in the land, they began to conquer their enemies. The territory, in which they gained, however, was far short of what God had promised them. Their own sin, as well as complacency, kept them from inhabiting the entire Land of Promise.

The Tabernacle and the Ark of the Covenant eventually came to rest at Shiloh, some 25 miles north of Jerusalem. This home for the sacred object was only temporary. After staying in Shiloh for over 400 years, the time had come for a permanent home for the Ark to be built. This would be on the specific spot which God alone would determine.

THE REIGN OF DAVID

One of the greatest figures in the history of Israel was David—a shepherd boy that God made king. David captured the city of Jerusalem from the Jebusites, and made it Israel's capital. David then brought the Ark of the Covenant to Jerusalem, and placed it in the Tabernacle.

King David observed that while he lived in a house of cedar, a palace, God's symbolic presence, the Ark of the Covenant, was still residing in a tent (the Tabernacle). Hence, David conceived a plan for a more permanent structure to be built, a Temple.

THE TEMPLE WILL BE BUILT BY SOLOMON

God told David that a Temple was to be built, but not by him. David was not to be the one who would build this holy structure because he was a man of war. That job would belong to his son, Solomon. The original command for building the Temple was given by God to David. The Lord said, "He shall build a house for my name" (2 Samuel 7:13). Solomon, not David, would build the Temple.

THE TEMPLE SITE IS CHOSEN BY GOD

The specific place for the site of the Temple was chosen by God before the reign of Solomon. We read the following in the Book of Second Samuel.

> So the LORD sent a plague on Israel from that morning until the end of the time designated, and seventy thousand of the people from Dan to Beersheba died. When the angel stretched out his hand to destroy Jerusalem, the LORD relented concerning the disaster and said to the angel who was afflicting the people, "Enough! Withdraw your hand." The angel of the LORD was then at the threshing floor of Araunah the Jebusite. When David saw the angel who was striking down the people, he said to the LORD, "I have sinned; I, the shepherd, have done wrong. These are but sheep. What have they done? Let your hand fall on me and my family." On that day Gad went to David and said to him, "Go up and build an altar to the LORD on the threshing

floor of Araunah the Jebusite.") . . . . David built an altar to the LORD there and sacrificed burnt offerings and fellowship offerings. Then the LORD answered his prayer in behalf of the land, and the plague on Israel was stopped (2 Samuel 24:15-18,25 NIV).

King David purchased the threshing floor of Araunah as the site of the First Temple. There he built an altar and offered a sacrifice at the exact place that God had designated. The spot was on Mt. Moriah— the same mountain range where one thousand years earlier God had stopped Abraham from sacrificing Isaac.

THE BUILDING OF THE FIRST TEMPLE

After the death of his father David, Solomon ordered the building of the First Temple. Solomon said.

> You know that because of the wars waged against my father David from all sides, he could not build a temple for the Name of the LORD his God until the LORD put his enemies under his feet (1 Kings 5:3 NIV).

The Bible says that Solomon began to build the Temple in the fourth year of his reign.

> In the four hundred and eightieth year after the Israelites came out of Egypt, in the fourth year of Solomon's reign over Israel, in the month of Ziv, the second month, he began to build the temple of the LORD (1 Kings 6:1 NIV).

The building of Solomon's Temple was a huge undertaking. Craftsmen from Tyre and Sidon were employed to build this magnificent structure. Construction took seven years. The Bible says.

> King Solomon conscripted laborers from all Israel—thirty thousand men . . . He conscripted 70,000 men as carriers

and 80,000 as stonecutters in the hills and 3,600 as foremen over them (1 Kings 5:13; 2 Chronicles 2:2 NIV).

The stones were hewn from a quarry and brought to the Temple site. Scripture says.

> In building the temple, only blocks dressed at the quarry were used, and no hammer, chisel or any other iron tool was heard at the temple site while it was being built (1 Kings 6:7 NIV).

The sound of the hammer or chisel was not heard in the Temple area while this magnificent structure was being constructed.

THE TEMPLE WAS DEDICATED TO THE LORD

After its completion in 953 B.C., King Solomon dedicated the Temple. In his prayer Solomon recognized that the Temple was not the dwelling place of God, but only representative of His presence.

> But will God really dwell on earth? The heavens, even the highest heaven, cannot contain you. How much less this temple I have built! (1 Kings 8:27 NIV).

The Temple, therefore, was not built to house His presence. Indeed, God certainly did not need it to exist.

THE TEMPLE WAS FREE FROM IDOLS

The feature that set apart the Solomonic Temple from other temples in the ancient world is that there were no idols in it. The Holy of Holies contained only the Ark of the Covenant—the object that contained God's commandments for His people.

One thousand years after the Temple's construction, Stephen, the first martyr of the Christian church, recognized this. He said the following words to an antagonistic crowd.

But it was Solomon who built a house for him. However, the Most High does not live in houses made by human hands. As the prophet says: 'Heaven is my throne, and the earth is my footstool. What kind of house will you build for me? says the Lord. Or where will my resting place be? Has not my hand made all these things?' (Acts 7:47-50 NIV).

The construction of the Temple brought to a close the history of the Tabernacle. Permanent changes were then made in the worship of the people. Indeed, as He had promised, the Lord brought His people to this special land, the Promised Land, as well as to a precise place where a sanctuary, a Temple would be built.

SUMMARY TO CHAPTER 4

With the city of Jerusalem under the control of Abraham's descendants, God ordered a permanent home for the Ark to be constructed. The Ark of the Covenant would be mobile no longer. The Temple site, chosen by God, was on the same mountain where a thousand years earlier Abraham was kept from sacrificing Isaac—perhaps on the exact spot.

Under Solomon's rule, the magnificent Temple was built, the Ark had found a home, and the people were at peace. The promises of God were fulfilled.

However, this great time of blessing around the Temple would be short-lived. Sin was about to take its toll.

CHAPTER 5

The First Temple is Destroyed as Predicted: The People are Sent in Exile

How deserted lies the city, once so full of people! How like a widow is she, who once was great among the nations! She who was queen among the provinces has now become a slave. Bitterly she weeps at night, tears are on her cheeks. Among all her lovers there is no one to comfort her. All her friends have betrayed her; they have become her enemies. After affliction and harsh labor, Judah has gone into exile. She dwells among the nations; she finds no resting place. All who pursue her have overtaken her in the midst of her distress.

(Lamentations of Jeremiah 1:1-3)

Before the children of Israel had entered into the Promised Land, God reconfirmed the covenant with them that He had made with Abraham. Moses recorded the Lord saying.

See, I have given you this land. Go in and take possession of the land that the LORD swore he would give to your fathers—to Abraham, Isaac and Jacob—and to their descendants after them (Deuteronomy 1:8).

The Promised Land was theirs for the taking.

THERE WILL BE BLESSINGS FOR OBEDIENCE

God promised the nation a series of blessings if they would be obedient to Him. We read about this in Deuteronomy. It says.

> If you fully obey the LORD your God and carefully follow all his commands I give you today, the LORD your God will set you high above all the nations on earth. All these blessings will come on you and accompany you if you obey the LORD your God (Deuteronomy 28:1-2 NIV).

God would bless the nation as long as they fully obeyed.

THERE WILL BE PUNISHMENT FOR DISOBEDIENCE

Yet, warnings of punishment were also given to the people if they disobeyed the Lord. We also read in Deuteronomy.

> However, if you do not obey the LORD your God and do not carefully follow all his commands and decrees I am giving you today, all these curses will come on you and overtake you. . . Then the LORD will scatter you among all nations, from one end of the earth to the other. There you will worship other gods—gods of wood and stone, which neither you nor your ancestors have known (Deuteronomy 28:15,64 NIV).

Therefore, disobedience will bring judgment from the Lord.

GOD'S MERCY WILL BE SHOWN

God, because of His great mercy, then promised to bring the scattered people back to their land. The Bible says.

> When all these things happen to you—the blessings and curses I have set before you—and you come to your senses while you are in all the nations where the Lord your God has driven you, and you and your children return to the Lord

your God and obey Him with all your heart and all your soul by doing everything I am giving you today, then He will restore your fortunes, have compassion on you, and gather you again from all the peoples where the Lord your God has scattered you (Deuteronomy 30:1-3 HCSB).

From these verses we can observe the following predictions.

1. As long as the people would remain faithful to Him, God would bless them as well as give them victory over their enemies.

2. However, God would remove them from the land if they were unfaithful to Him.

3. God, in His faithfulness, did promise to bring them back into the land to keep the terms of His covenant with Abraham.

The history of the nation Israel is a testimony to the fulfillment of the promises, of both the blessings, and the punishments.

THE KINGDOM WAS DIVIDED INTO NORTH AND SOUTH

As King Solomon advanced in years, his spiritual life declined. He made unwise political alliances by marrying foreign wives. Solomon went further by allowing the people to worship the gods of his pagan wives. These wives brought in their idols to Jerusalem—to the very precincts of the Temple. This set the stage for the dividing of the kingdom.

Unfortunately, the nation was on the same spiritual decline as Solomon. When Solomon died his son Rehoboam became king of Israel. Rehoboam's policies caused the kingdom to be divided into north (Israel) and south (Judah). The northern kingdom consisted of ten tribes while the southern kingdom had only two tribes, Judah and Benjamin.

THERE WAS A SUBSTITUTE PLACE OF WORSHIP BUILT

Jeroboam, the first king of Israel, built two substitute places of worship, one in Bethel and one in Dan. He did this for fear the people would return to Jerusalem, and worship in the Temple. We read about what took place.

> Jeroboam said to himself, "The way things are going now, the kingdom might return to the house of David. If these people regularly go to offer sacrifices in the Lord's temple in Jerusalem, the heart of these people will return to their lord, Rehoboam king of Judah. They will murder me and go back to the king of Judah." So the king sought advice. Then he made two golden calves, and he said to the people, "Going to Jerusalem is too difficult for you. Israel, here is your God who brought you out of the land of Egypt, He set up one in Bethel, and put the other in Dan. This led to sin; the people walked in procession before one of the calves all the way to Dan (1 Kings 12:26-29 HCSB).

Interestingly, the ruins of the altar, and the temple that Jeroboam built in Dan, exist to this day.

THE NORTHERN KINGDOM WAS TAKEN CAPTIVE

The northern kingdom remained in idolatry until its captivity in 721 B.C. by the Assyrians. The kingdom was never restored. The entire history of the northern kingdom of Israel was characterized by idolatry.

THE SOUTHERN KINGDOM ALSO FELL INTO SIN

The southern kingdom of Judah did not fare much better. They too fell into sin. The history of the kingdom of Judah, and the First Temple in Jerusalem, is covered in the books of the Kings and Chronicles. We will consider some of the most important events that deal specifically with the Temple.

THE TEMPLE TREASURES WERE TAKEN

During the reign of Rehoboam, God permitted Pharaoh Shishak of Egypt to plunder the Temple. We read about this in Second Chronicles.

Because they had been unfaithful to the LORD, Shishak king of Egypt attacked Jerusalem in the fifth year of King Rehoboam . . . When Shishak king of Egypt attacked Jerusalem, he carried off the treasures of the temple of the LORD and the treasures of the royal palace. He took everything, including the gold shields Solomon had made (2 Chronicles 12:2,9 NIV).

This was the first of a series of sieges against Jerusalem.

AHAZ DESECRATES THE TEMPLE

Later in Judah's history an evil King named Ahaz defiled the Temple. The Bible says that he desecrated the Temple, and stole its treasures. Ahaz then sent the Temple treasures to Assyria to make an alliance against Israel and Syria. Ahaz then went to Damascus and had a copy of their pagan altar made. He then brought it to Jerusalem, replaced the altar of the Lord with this pagan replica, and offered sacrifices upon it. Ahaz also closed the Temple and broke up the vessels.

HEZEKIAH REPAIRS THE TEMPLE

King Hezekiah, the next king of Judah, repaired the damages made by Ahaz.

Hezekiah was 25 years old when he became king and reigned 29 years in Jerusalem. His mother's name was Abijah daughter of Zechariah. He did what was right in the Lord's sight just as his ancestor David had done. In the first year of his reign, in the first month, he opened the doors of the Lord's temple and repaired them (2 Chronicles 29:1-3 HCSB).

Though Hezekiah was a good king, he and the people of Jerusalem were lifted up with pride. This assured the eventual destruction of Jerusalem and the Temple. We read about this in Second Chronicles.

> In those days Hezekiah became ill and was at the point of death. He prayed to the LORD, who answered him and gave him a miraculous sign. But Hezekiah's heart was proud and he did not respond to the kindness shown him; therefore the LORD's wrath was on him and on Judah and Jerusalem. Then Hezekiah repented of the pride of his heart, as did the people of Jerusalem; therefore the LORD's wrath did not come on them during the days of Hezekiah (2 Chronicles 32:24-26 NIV).

Hezekiah's humbling of himself only postponed the inevitable downfall of Judah, Jerusalem and the Temple.

IDOLATRY WAS ON THE INCREASE AMONG THE PEOPLE

The humility of the king and the people was short-lived. Hezekiah's son, Manasseh, built pagan altars in the Temple courts, and placed an idolatrous image in the Temple. God punished Manasseh by sending him to Babylon. When Manasseh repented, he was returned to Jerusalem, where he repaired the altar.

Manasseh's son, Amon, following in the idolatrous example of his father. However, his reign did not last long. After two years Amon's servants assassinated him. The people then killed the assassins and made Josiah king.

THERE WAS A REFORMATION UNDER KING JOSIAH

The Temple was restored under the leadership of Josiah. He, like Hezekiah, commanded that the damaged Temple should be repaired. We read the following.

> In the eighteenth year of King Josiah, the king sent the court secretary Shaphan son of Azaliah, son of Meshullam, to the Lord's temple, saying, "Go up to Hilkiah the high priest so that he may total up the money brought into the Lord's

temple—the money the doorkeepers have collected from the people. It is to be put into the hands of those doing the work—those who oversee the Lord's temple. They in turn are to give it to the workmen in the Lord's temple to repair the damage (2 Kings 22:3-5 HCSB).

King Josiah also removed the idols from the Temple and restored two of the Temple's courts. He also ordered the Ark of the Covenant to be put back into the Holy of Holies.

He said to the Levites, who instructed all Israel and who had been consecrated to the LORD: "Put the sacred ark in the temple that Solomon son of David king of Israel built. It is not to be carried about on your shoulders. Now serve the LORD your God and his people Israel" (2 Chronicles 35:3 NIV).

The people, however, did not truly turn to the Lord in repentance.

THE DESTRUCTION OF THE TEMPLE WAS FORETOLD

The prophets predicted the certain destruction of the Temple. The prophet Micah said of Jerusalem, the Temple, and the Temple Mount.

Therefore because of you, Zion will be plowed like a field, Jerusalem will become a heap of rubble, the temple hill a mound overgrown with thickets (Micah 3:12 NIV).

Likewise, the prophet Jeremiah said.

And if you do not listen to the words of my servants the prophets, whom I have sent to you again and again (though you have not listened), then I will make this house like Shiloh and this city a curse among all the nations of the earth (Jeremiah 26:5-6 NIV).

Jeremiah's reference to Shiloh concerned the place where the Ark of the Covenant had previously resided. As Shiloh was in ruins, so would be Jerusalem and the Temple.

THE PEOPLE WERE SENT INTO CAPTIVITY

In addition, the prophet Jeremiah also predicted a seventy-year captivity of the people for their sins against the Lord. Furthermore, he pronounced judgment on those who would destroy her, Babylon. We read.

> This whole country will become a desolate wasteland, and these nations will serve the king of Babylon seventy years. "But when the seventy years are fulfilled, I will punish the king of Babylon and his nation, the land of the Babylonians, for their guilt," declares the LORD, "and will make it desolate forever" (Jeremiah 25:11-12 NIV).

The people did not believe Jeremiah. They could not conceive that the Lord would allow His holy Temple to be destroyed. How wrong they were! Destruction was soon to occur.

THE TEMPLE VESSELS WERE TAKEN

The reign of Jehoiakim (610 B.C.) was the beginning of the end for Judah. Nebuchadnezzar, king of Babylon, made Jehoiakim his subject. After three years of being his vassal, Jehoiakim rebelled.

> During Jehoiakim's reign, Nebuchadnezzar king of Babylon attacked. Jehoiakim became his vassal for three years, and then he turned and rebelled against him. The Lord sent Chaldean, Aramean, Moabite, and Ammonite raiders against Jehoiakim. He sent them against Judah to destroy it, according to the word of the Lord He had spoken through His servants the prophets. Indeed, this happened to Judah at the Lord's command to remove them from His sight. It was because of the sins of Manasseh, according to all he had done, and also because of all the innocent blood he had shed. He had filled Jerusalem with innocent blood, and the Lord would not forgive (2 Kings 24:1-4 HCSB).

God allowed these raiding bands to judge Jehoiakim. The king died, but the rebellion continued.

THE CITY WAS PLACED UNDER SIEGE

His son Jehoiachin also did evil. Nebuchadnezzar then laid siege to the city. The Bible says.

> At that time the officers of Nebuchadnezzar king of Babylon advanced on Jerusalem and laid siege to it (2 Kings 24:10 NIV).

Jehoiachin and his family were taken prisoner to Babylon along with ten thousand captives. The Temple vessels were also taken to Babylon. Only the poorest of the poor remained in the land.

THE FIRST TEMPLE WAS DESTROYED AS PREDICTED

The destruction of Jerusalem and the First Temple was carried out as predicted. We read about this in the Book of Second Kings. It says.

> On the seventh day of the fifth month, in the nineteenth year of Nebuchadnezzar king of Babylon, Nebuzaradan commander of the imperial guard, an official of the king of Babylon, came to Jerusalem. He set fire to the temple of the LORD, the royal palace and all the houses of Jerusalem. Every important building he burned down. The whole Babylonian army under the commander of the imperial guard broke down the walls around Jerusalem. Nebuzaradan the commander of the guard carried into exile the people who remained in the city, along with the rest of the populace and those who had deserted to the king of Babylon (2 Kings 25:8-12 NIV).

Nebuchadnezzar, the king of Babylon, destroyed the city and Temple in 587 B.C., as the prophets had predicted. The magnificent Temple was destroyed, and the Ark of the Covenant, the most sacred object ever constructed, disappeared from history. To this day its fate remains unknown.

THERE ARE ONLY A FEW REMAINS LEFT

The destruction of the First Temple and the ravages of time have left few remains of Solomon's magnificent structure. Archaeologist Eilat Mazar made the following observations.

> For ten years—from 1968 to 1977—the area adjacent to the southern wall of Jerusalem's Temple Mount was intensively excavated. Astounding discoveries were made, but hardly a trace of anything from the First Temple period was uncovered . . . In ten years of excavation . . . only the scantiest First Temple remains were found. It eventually became clear that intensive quarrying over a period of 1,500 years (since the Babylonian destruction of Solomon's Temple) had left nothing from the First Temple period except a few trace walls and pockets of finds of little informative value. Approximately 350 years of First Temple development and construction appeared to be lost to archaeologists.[1]

While there seems to be little physical evidence of the First Temple that still remains this has not stopped people from attempting to discover the exact site where it stood. As we shall see, this quest will have significant meaning in the future.

SUMMARY TO CHAPTER 5

The First Temple existed for a relatively short period of time (less than 400 years). Though the people were punished for their sin, and expelled from their land, God, who is rich in mercy, promised them they would return.

The exile from the land would be short-lived, because the promises of God would again be fulfilled.

---

1. Eilat Mazar, Royal Gateway To Ancient Jerusalem Uncovered, *Biblical Archaeology Review*, May/June 1989, pp. 38, 40

CHAPTER 6

God's Promises Come True: The Jews Return from Exile and a Second Temple Is Built

> This is what the LORD says—your Redeemer, who formed
> you in the womb: I am the LORD, the Maker of all things,
> who stretches out the heavens, who spreads out the earth by
> myself, who foils the signs of false prophets and makes fools
> of diviners, who overthrows the learning of the wise and
> turns it into nonsense, who carries out the words of his ser-
> vants and fulfills the predictions of his messengers, who says
> of Jerusalem, 'It shall be inhabited' of the towns of Judah,
> 'They shall be rebuilt,' and of their ruins, 'I will restore them.'
> The Lord God (Isaiah 44:24-26)

The land lay desolate, Jerusalem was in rubble, the magnificent Temple that Solomon had built had been destroyed, and the people were taken into captivity by the Babylonians. From the outside, the situation looked hopeless for the people of Judah.

Nevertheless, the Bible records that people still came to Jerusalem to offer sacrifices. We read the following in the Book of Jeremiah.

> The day after Gedaliah's assassination, before anyone knew
> about it, eighty men who had shaved off their beards, torn
> their clothes and cut themselves came from Shechem, Shiloh
> and Samaria, bringing grain offerings and incense with them
> to the house of the LORD (Jeremiah 41:4-5 NIV).

Yet there was no Temple in which they could offer their sacrifices. Seemingly all was lost.

THERE WAS HOPE FOR A RETURN

But the people were not without hope. The Lord had predicted the destruction of the city of Jerusalem and the Temple, as well as the captivity.

However, that was not all that was predicted! The Lord said, through the prophets, that the people would return to their land, and rebuild their city and Temple. As is always the case, the predictions of the Lord came to pass.

DANIEL'S READS JEREMIAH'S PROPHECY

The prophet Daniel, while in captivity in Babylon, read the prophecies of Jeremiah concerning the predicted return from captivity.

> In the first year of Darius son of Xerxes (a Mede by descent), who was made ruler over the Babylonian kingdom—in the first year of his reign, I, Daniel, understood from the Scriptures, according to the word of the LORD given to Jeremiah the prophet, that the desolation of Jerusalem would last seventy years (Daniel 9:1,2 NIV).

Daniel realized the seventy years were about fulfilled, and that the return from captivity was at hand.

THE AMAZING PROPHECY ABOUT KING CYRUS

This brings us to one of the most amazing prophecies in the entire Bible. It concerns the return of the Jews from captivity, and the building of the Second Temple, as well as the city of Jerusalem.

Isaiah the prophet, writing in 700 B.C., recorded the Lord saying the following things.

This is what the LORD says—your Redeemer, who formed you in the womb: I am the LORD, the Maker of all things, who stretches out the heavens, who spreads out the earth by myself who carries out the words of his servants and fulfills the predictions of his messengers, who says of Jerusalem, 'It shall be inhabited,' of the towns of Judah, "They shall be rebuilt,' and of their ruins, 'I will restore them,' who says to the watery deep, 'Be dry, and I will dry up your streams,' who says of Cyrus, 'He is my shepherd and will accomplish all that I please; he will say of Jerusalem, "Let it be rebuilt," and of the temple, "Let its foundations be laid." This is what the LORD says to his anointed, to Cyrus, whose right hand I take hold of to subdue nations before him and to strip kings of their armor, to open doors before him so that gates will not be shut: I will go before you and will level the mountains; I will break down gates of bronze and cut through bars of iron. I will give you hidden treasures, riches stored in secret places, so that you may know that I am the LORD, the God of Israel, who summons you by name. For the sake of Jacob my servant, of Israel my chosen, I summon you by name and bestow on you a title of honor, though you do not acknowledge me (Isaiah 44:26-45:4 NIV).

From this passage we can see the following specific predictions.

1. The southern kingdom of Judah would return from captivity.

2. The rebuilding of the city of Jerusalem would begin.

3. The foundation of the Second Temple would be laid.

4. All this would be accomplished by a man named Cyrus who is addressed by name.

5. King Cyrus will do this even though he was not a believer in the God of Israel.

According to Isaiah's prophecy, Cyrus would be the person the Lord stirred up. He was the one who would perform this task of the Lord even though he did not personally know Him. Cyrus was merely an instrument in God's plan.

THE TEMPLE WAS STILL STANDING WHEN THIS PROPHECY WAS GIVEN

When the prophecy of Isaiah was given, the Temple was still standing, the city of Jerusalem had not yet been destroyed, and the people were not yet in exile. Furthermore, Cyrus hadn't even been born! Incredibly, all these predictions were literally fulfilled as Isaiah prophesied.

THE PEOPLE RETURN AS PREDICTED

Almost two hundred years after the prophecy was given, the return of the Jews was indeed granted by a decree of a Persian King named Cyrus. The Book of Ezra records the fulfillment.

> This is what Cyrus king of Persia says: The LORD, the God of heaven, has given me all the kingdoms of the earth and he has appointed me to build a temple for him at Jerusalem in Judah. Any of his people among you may go up to Jerusalem in Judah and build the temple of the LORD, the God of Israel, the God who is in Jerusalem, and may their God be with them (Ezra 1:2,3 NIV).

There is evidence, apart from the Bible, that Cyrus was aware of the prophecies. The first-century Jewish writer Flavius Josephus writes.

> By reading the book which Isaiah left behind of his prophecies; for this prophet said that God had spoken thus to him in a secret vision—'My will is, that Cyrus, whom I have appointed to be king over many and great nations, send back my people to their own land, and build my Temple.' Accordingly, when Cyrus read this, and admired the divine

power, an earnest desire and ambition seized upon him to fulfill what was so written.[1]

Consequently, Cyrus knew that the Lord was indeed God!

THE LAND GETS ITS REST

Seventy years after the inhabitants of Jerusalem were taken to Babylon, the command was given for them to return to their land. The prophecy of Jeremiah was literally fulfilled. For seventy years, the people were removed from the land for neglecting to give it rest. The Bible says.

> This whole country will become a desolate wasteland, and these nations will serve the king of Babylon seventy years. But when the seventy years are fulfilled, I will punish the king of Babylon and his nation, the land of the Babylonians, for their guilt, declares the LORD, and will make it desolate forever (Jeremiah 25:11-12 NIV).

The Scriptures commanded that every seventh year the land should be allowed to rest. The people, however, ignored this command. For 490 consecutive years, they worked the land without giving it the commanded rest. This meant that during this period there should have been seventy years in which the land was made to rest. Because the people did not observe those seventy years, God took them away from the land for that exact period of time to fulfill His commandment! The Scripture makes it clear that this was one of the reasons for the Babylonian captivity.

The Babylonians set fire to God's temple and broke down the walls of Jerusalem. They also burned all the palaces and destroyed everything of value there. The Bible says of Nebuchadnezzar.

> He carried into exile to Babylon the remnant, who escaped from the sword, and they became servants to him and his

---

1. Flavius Josephus, *Antiquities*, Book XI, Chapter 1:2

successors until the kingdom of Persia came to power. The land enjoyed its sabbath rests; all the time of its desolation it rested, until the seventy years were completed in fulfillment of the word of the LORD spoken by Jeremiah (2 Chronicles 36:19-21 NIV).

THE CAMPAIGN TO REBUILD THE TEMPLE

After the Jews returned to Jerusalem, a campaign was begun to rebuild the Temple. The prophet Haggai said.

> This is what the LORD Almighty says: "These people say, 'The time has not yet come to rebuild the LORD's house.'" Then the word of the LORD came through the prophet Haggai: "Is it a time for you yourselves to be living in your paneled houses, while this house remains a ruin?" . . . "Go up into the mountains and bring down timber and build the house, so that I may take pleasure in it and be honored," says the LORD (Haggai 1:2-4,8 NIV).

The rebuilding of the Temple was started in Cyrus' reign. The Bible records what occurred.

> In the second month of the second year after their arrival at the house of God in Jerusalem, Zerubbabel son of Shealtiel, Joshua son of Jozadak and the rest of the people (the priests and the Levites and all who had returned from the captivity to Jerusalem) began the work, appointing Levites twenty years old and older to supervise the building of the house of the LORD. Joshua and his sons and brothers and Kadmiel and his sons (descendants of Hodaviah and the sons of Henadad and their sons and brothers—all Levites—joined together in supervising those working on the house of God. When the builders laid the foundation of the temple of the LORD, the priests in their vestments and with trumpets,

and the Levites (the sons of Asaph) with cymbals, took their places to praise the LORD, as prescribed by David king of Israel. With praise and thanksgiving they sang to the LORD: "He is good; his love toward Israel endures forever." And all the people gave a great shout of praise to the LORD, because the foundation of the house of the LORD was laid (Ezra 3:8-11 NIV).

The Temple was rebuilt as the Lord had predicted.

ZERUBBABEL AND JOSHUA LEAD THE PEOPLE

Under the leadership of two men, Zerubbabel and Joshua, the work of rebuilding started. The altar was rebuilt and the Temple service was renewed. Those who returned, however, ran into various difficulties. These came mainly from the recent settlers in the land who were united in their opposition to the returning Jews. The Bible says.

> When the enemies of Judah and Benjamin heard that the exiles were building a temple for the LORD, the God of Israel, Then the peoples around them set out to discourage the people of Judah and make them afraid to go on building. They bribed officials to work against them and frustrate their plans during the entire reign of Cyrus king of Persia and down to the reign of Darius king of Persia (Ezra 4:1,4,5 NIV).

It would be some decades later, under the leadership of Ezra and Nehemiah, that Jerusalem was finally reconstructed and the walls of the Temple rebuilt.

THE TEMPLE WAS BUILT UPON THE SAME HOLY SITE

The Second Temple was built upon the exact site on the Temple Mount as Solomon's Temple. There were some old men, who had actually seen the First Temple, and thus could help the builders with their task.

The entire site of the Temple was still considered holy. Laymen were forbidden to enter the Temple area. When Nehemiah was advised to seek refuge in the Temple to hide from those seeking his life he replied.

> But I said, "Should someone like me run away? Or should one like me go into the temple to save his life? I will not go!" (Nehemiah 6:11 NIV).

The holiness of the Temple was an accepted fact.

THE SECOND TEMPLE WAS FINALLY COMPLETED

Though Cyrus gave the decree for the restoration of Jerusalem, and the rebuilding of the Temple, he did not live to see either task completed. Two Persian kings, Darius (522-486 B.C.), and Artaxerxes I (465-423 B.C.), the successors of Cyrus, saw through the completion of the rebuilding of the city and the Temple.

The Second Temple was finally completed in 517 B.C. under the leadership of Zerubbabel, and inspired by the prophet Haggai. The Book of Ezra records the following.

> The temple was completed on the third day of the month Adar, in the sixth year of the reign of King Darius. Then the people of Israel—the priests, the Levites and the rest of the exiles—celebrated the dedication of the house of God with joy (Ezra 6:15,16 NIV).

Though there was rejoicing at the new Temple, those who had seen the glory of the previous one were moved to tears.

> But many of the older priests and Levites and family heads, who had seen the former temple, wept aloud when they saw the foundation of this temple being laid, while many others shouted for joy (Ezra 3:12 NIV).

By comparison, the Second Temple was much inferior in its magnificence to the previous Temple. God, however, was pleased with this new structure. The prophet Haggai had predicted the Second Temple's glory would be greater than the first.

> The glory of this present house will be greater than the glory of the former house, says the LORD Almighty. And in this place I will grant peace, declares the LORD Almighty (Haggai 2:9 NIV).

The reason was not the size of the building, because in that respect, the Second Temple was inferior to the First. The greater glory in the Second Temple was that the promised Messiah eventually came to it.

THERE WERE THINGS MISSING FROM THE NEW TEMPLE

This new Temple was lacking certain valuable things that the First Temple contained. These included: The Shekinah glory, the holy fire, the Urim and Thummim, and the Ark of the Covenant. Though the Ark was missing, the holiness of the site was still there. We read.

> To be sure the Holy of Holies in the Second Temple was empty; the Ark, Cherubim, and . . . Mercy Seat . . . of the First Temple were never replaced. Only the projection of bare rock, known as "The Foundation Stone," served as a reminder that this was where the Ark of the Covenant had once stood. Nonetheless, the holiness of the place remained unimpaired.[2]

Unfortunately, there is little known about the Temple built by Zerubbabel. It is difficult to determine, even in general outline, the stages in the historical development of the Temple Mount and its fortifications, during this time.

---

2. Jacob Milgrom, Challenge to Sun-Worship Interpretation of Temple Scroll's Gilded Staircase, *Biblical Archaeology Review*, January/February 1975 p. 72

SUMMARY TO CHAPTER 6

Though the first Temple was destroyed, Jerusalem was in rubble, the land desolate, and the people were exiled to Babylon, God would not allow that situation to last. Through the prophets Isaiah and Jeremiah, before any of these things took place, the Lord predicted the return of the people to the land, the rebuilding of the desolate places, and the rebuilding of Jerusalem and the Temple

God's Word did come to pass, and the people built a Second Temple. Idolatry was a thing of the past. There would, however, be other obstacles the people would have to face, and the future would bring new challenges to the sacred city, and the Holy Temple.

CHAPTER 7

The Second Temple Is Defiled by Invaders: The Temple Is Later Enlarged by Herod

> Pompey was the first Roman who subdued the Jews. By right
> of conquest he entered their temple. It is a fact well known,
> that he found no image, no statue, no symbolical representa-
> tion of the Deity: the whole presented a naked dome; the
> sanctuary was unadorned and simple. By Pompey's orders
> the walls of the city were leveled to the ground, but the tem-
> ple was left entire.
>
> Tacitus (Historiae, 5, 9:1)

After its construction and dedication, the Second Temple functioned
for several hundred years without any major incidents. Then trouble
struck. The Temple fell prey to foreign powers which defiled its holiness. The Holy of Holies was entered on two occasions by foreign
invaders.

THE DESECRATION OF ANTIOCHUS IV

The Second Temple was desecrated in 167 B.C. by a Seleucid ruler
named Antiochus IV. Antiochus took upon himself the name
Epiphanes ("coming"). The Book of 1 Maccabees records some of
Antiochus' deeds.

> He engaged King Ptolemy of Egypt in battle, and Ptolemy
> turned and fled before him, and many were wounded and

fell. They captured the fortified cities in the land of Egypt, and he plundered the land of Egypt. After subduing Egypt, Antiochus returned in the one hundred forty-third year. He went up against Israel and came to Jerusalem with a strong force. He arrogantly entered the sanctuary and took the golden altar, the lampstand for the light, and all its utensils (1 Maccabees 1:18-21 NRSV).

Antiochus laid siege to Jerusalem and took it. He killed thousands of its inhabitants, and captured and sold many more for slaves. Antiochus came to the Temple, and defiled it. In fact, this evil person desecrated the Lord's Temple by slaughtering a pig on the altar, and then placing a pagan image in the Holy of Holies.

Antiochus also carried away the Temple treasures. Several years later, he forbade the people to sacrifice to the Lord. In addition, the Books of the Law were torn in pieces and burned. He set up altars and idols throughout the land.

ANTIOCHUS ORDERED DEATH FOR DISOBEDIENCE

A command was given that whoever did not obey the king's orders would die. Antiochus threatened that he would gather the entire Jewish nation into Jerusalem, destroy every one of them, and make Jerusalem the place of their mass grave. Before his threat was accomplished, Antiochus was struck with an incurable disease. He died in agony, attributing his dying torments to the God whose religion he had insulted, and whose people and Temple he had defiled. And yet, it appears from the Rosetta stone, that, he was worshipped as a god after his death.

THE MACCABEAN REVOLT

In 165 B.C., a revolt was led by Judas Maccabaeus to cleanse the defiled Temple. The revolt succeeded and the Temple was purified. The Book of First Maccabees records the event.

Then said Judas and his brothers, "Behold, our enemies are crushed; let us go up to cleanse the sanctuary and dedicate it." So all the army assembled and they went up to Mount Zion. And they saw the sanctuary desolate, the altar profaned, and the gates burned. In the courts they saw bushes sprung up as in a thicket, or as on one of the mountains. They saw also the chambers of the priests in ruins. Then they rent their clothes, and mourned with great lamentation, and sprinkled themselves with ashes. They fell face down on the ground, and sounded the signal on the trumpets, and cried out to Heaven (1 Maccabees 4:36-40 NRSV).

THE REFURNISHING OF THE DEFILED TEMPLE IS DESCRIBED

The apocryphal book of First Maccabees provides details of the refurnishing of the Second Temple by these heroes. It says.

They made new holy vessels, and brought the lampstand, the altar of incense, and the table into the temple. Then they offered incense on the altar and lit the lamps on the lampstand, and these gave light in the temple (1 Maccabees 4:49,50 NRSV).

Consequently, the Temple was once again furnished. The Jews, with the yearly celebration of Hanukkah, remember this cleansing and rededication of the Temple.

THE HASMONEAN CONSTRUCTION

From 165 B.C. to 63 B.C., the descendants of the Maccabees, the Hasmoneans, ruled from an independent Jerusalem. Under the Hasmoneans, further construction was carried out on the Temple.

When . . . Israel had been under foreign rule, further building had not been allowed at the Temple site. The rulers had forbidden any extension of the existing Temple edifice.

Now under the Hasmonean kings, the Jews could—and did glorify and exalt the House of God and the mountain on which it stood. The Temple Mount area was rehabilitated and reconstructed most firmly. Vestiges of this activity exist today in the eastern wall of the Temple Mount.[1]

ROME INVADES THE HOLY LAND

One hundred years later, in 63 B.C, Israel came under the control of Rome when the Roman General Pompey captured the city of Jerusalem. When Pompey arrived at the Temple, he found the Holy of Holies empty.

HEROD THE GREAT BUILDER

In 37 B.C. the Romans appointed Herod the Great, a non-Jew, as king over Israel. Herod convened a national assembly in 20 B.C. in which he presented a plan for an enlargement of the Temple. Herod proposed to build the Temple to the same specifications as the one built by Solomon. He told the people that this new Temple would be more worthy of the name of their God. Hence an enlargement of the Second Temple was undertaken during the reign of Herod. This enlargement of the Second Temple became known as "Herod's Temple."

The irony is that Herod was an evil man with no religious faith whatsoever. He did not care for the Jews, or for the God of Israel. In fact, the Temple in Jerusalem is not all that he built. Indeed, at this same time he also built a temple to the goddess Roma at Caesarea.

Furthermore, the appointments he made to the office of the High Priest were merely to further his own political aims. For example, in 36 B.C. Herod named his 17-year-old son-in-law Aristobulus III to be the High Priest. Yet, he murdered him the very next year. Then later in 23

---

1. Meir Ben Dov, *In The Shadow Of The Temple*, New York, Harper and Row, 1982. p. 23,24

B.C. this evil king married the high priest Simon's daughter. This was his third wife, whom he would also murder.

Why then did Herod oversee the expansion of the Temple? Most likely the reason he wanted to build a new Temple was as a memorial to perpetuate his name. Herod knew the people hated him, and that after his death he soon would be forgotten.

THE TEMPLE MOUNT WAS ENLARGED

Herod had to reconstruct the Temple that was already standing. The enlarged Temple was made twice the size as the First. Herod enlarged the Temple area by constructing a vast platform around it. The newly rebuilt Temple Mount was enormous. Archaeologist Meir Ben-Dov writes.

> The dimensions of the Temple Mount in Jerusalem, the largest site of its kind in the ancient world, were as follows: the southern wall, the shortest of the retaining walls, is 280 meters long; the eastern wall is 460 meters; the western and longest wall of the retaining walls is 485 meters; and the northern wall is 315 meters. The Temple Mount is therefore a trapezoid covering 144,000 square meters. Twelve soccer fields—bleachers included—would fit into this area![2]

JERUSALEM'S GLORY WAS GREAT

The glory of Jerusalem under Herod became well-known. The Babylonian Talmud said.

> Whoever has not seen Jerusalem in its splendor has never seen a lovely city (Babylonian Talmud).

Pliny the Elder, the famous Roman scholar, said the following of Jerusalem.

---

2. Meir Ben Dov, *In the Shadow of the Temple*, p. 24

[It is] by far the most renowned city of the Orient, and not of Judea only (Pliny the Elder)

Alfred Edersheim offers a fitting comment about Jerusalem and the Temple Mount, in the days of King Herod.

But alone, and isolated in its grandeur, stood the Temple Mount. Terrace upon terrace its courts rose, till, high above the city, within the enclosure of marble cloisters, cedar-roofed and richly ornamented, the Temple itself stood out a mass of snowy marble and of gold, glittering in the sunlight against the half-encircling green background of Olives. In all his wanderings the Jew had not seen such a city like his own Jerusalem. Not Antioch in Asia, not even Imperial Rome herself excelled in its architectural splendor. Nor has there been, either in ancient or modern times, a sacred building equal to the Temple, whether for situation or magnificence.[3]

JERUSALEM WAS WITHOUT IDOLS

One of the lessons the people of Israel had learned from the Babylonian captivity was to cease the worship of idols. The Roman writer Tacitus said of the Jews and Jerusalem.

The God of the Jews is a great governing mind that directs and guides the whole frame of nature, eternal, infinite, and neither capable of change, nor subject to decay. In consequence of this opinion, no such thing as a statue was to be seen in their city, much less in their temple.[4]

A ROMAN EAGLE WAS PLACED IN THE TEMPLE

Though Jerusalem was a city without idols, Herod, in an attempt to prove his loyalty to Rome, placed a statue of the Roman eagle above

---

3. Alfred Edersheim, *The Temple*, Grand Rapids, Michigan, Eerdmans, Reprinted 1992, p. 28
4. Tacitus, *Historiae*, 5, 9:1

the doorway of the Temple. By building the Temple, Herod showed his support of the Jews, when he placed the Roman eagle in the Temple, he showed his continued loyalty to Rome.

The Jews considered the Roman eagle a violation of the commandment against making any graven image. A riot occurred and the eagle was torn down and broken into pieces. Herod punished the violators, but only lived a few short months after this incident. In fact, Herod never lived to see his glorious building completed. His death was a sign to many that God was displeased with his profaning of the holy Temple.

SUMMARY TO CHAPTER 7

With the desecration by Antiochus, and the subjugation by Rome, the Second Temple had seen some difficult days. The enlargement of the Temple under Herod, along with his massive building program, made Jerusalem a magnificent city that even the Gentiles admired.

Yet the people were still under the yoke of Rome, and continued to pray for their promised Messiah. Their prayers were about to be answered. The fullness of time had come.

CHAPTER 8

The Messiah Comes and Is Rejected: Judgment Is Predicted Upon the Temple and the People

---

> I tell you that something greater than the temple is here
>
> Jesus (Matthew 12:6)

The Old Testament predicted a time when God would set up His kingdom in the person of a Deliverer known as "the Messiah." The Scripture promised that the Messiah would bring a time of peace to the world and would reign from Jerusalem in His Temple. The prophet Isaiah said.

> In the last days the mountain of the LORD's temple will be established as the highest of the mountains; it will be exalted above the hills, and all nations will stream to it. Many peoples will come and say, "Come, let us go up to the mountain of the LORD, to the temple of the God of Jacob. He will teach us his ways, so that we may walk in his paths." The law will go out from Zion, the word of the LORD from Jerusalem. He will judge between the nations and will settle disputes for many peoples. They will beat their swords into plowshares and their spears into pruning hooks. Nation will not take up sword against nation, nor will they train for war anymore (Isaiah 2:2-4 NIV).

The Messiah's coming is the hope of the Jewish people and of the entire world.

HE CAME AS PROMISED

The Messiah did come to Israel, and to the Temple, as God had promised. His name was Jesus of Nazareth. The Bible says.

> But when the appropriate time had come, God sent out his Son, born of a woman, born under the law, to redeem those who were under the law, so that we may be adopted as sons with full rights (Galatians 4:4,5 NET).

The fullness of time, or the "appropriate time," had indeed fully come.

JESUS AND THE TEMPLE

Important events in the life of Jesus Christ took place in the Temple area. To begin with, Jesus was brought to the Temple to be dedicated at the age of eight days. Luke records the following episode.

> So Simeon, directed by the Spirit, came into the temple courts, and when the parents brought in the child Jesus to do for him what was customary according to the law (Luke 2:27 NET).

When He was twelve, Luke records that Jesus confounded the elders with His wisdom while teaching in the Temple (Luke 2:41-50).

When Jesus was tempted by the devil, He was taken to the pinnacle of the Temple. This was, most likely, the same spot where the Apostle James was later martyred (Acts 12). Again we see that the Temple figured prominently in the life and ministry of Jesus.

JESUS WAS GREATER THAN THE TEMPLE

Jesus made some tremendous claims about Himself. One of the greatest of these concerned Himself and the Temple. The Bible records Jesus saying the following about His arrival.

I tell you that something greater than the temple is here (Matthew 12:6 NIV).

This claim placed Jesus' authority above that of the Temple.

JESUS CLEANSED THE TEMPLE

One of the most famous incidents in the life and ministry of Jesus took place in the Temple area. We read about this in the Gospel of John.

> The Jewish Passover was near, so Jesus went up to Jerusalem. In the temple complex He found people selling oxen, sheep, and doves, and He also found the money changers sitting there. After making a whip out of cords, He drove everyone out of the temple complex with their sheep and oxen. He also poured out the money changers' coins and overturned the tables. He told those who were selling doves, "Get these things out of here! Stop turning My Father's house into a marketplace" (John 2:13-16 HCSB).

The Temple was a place of prayer—it was not to be a place of business.

HE WAS DAILY TEACHING IN THE TEMPLE

Jesus spent considerable time teaching in the Temple. At his arrest, He emphasized that teaching in the Temple was something He did on a regular basis.

> In that hour Jesus said to the crowd, "Am I leading a rebellion, that you have come out with swords and clubs to capture me? Every day I sat in the temple courts teaching, and you did not arrest me" (Matthew 26:55 NIV).

The New Testament records various incidents of Jesus ministering and healing in the Temple. The Messiah had truly come to the Temple as promised.

JESUS WAS REJECTED BY THE PEOPLE OF ISRAEL

Unfortunately, His people rejected Him. The Bible records this sad event.

> He came to that which was his own, but his own did not receive him (John 1:11 NIV).

Because His own people rejected him, Jesus pronounced judgment upon Jerusalem, the Temple, and the people. Yet, the Lord also promised to return someday with the Temple figuring prominently into the last-days scenario.

THE DESTRUCTION OF THE SECOND TEMPLE IS PREDICTED

After the people rejected Jesus, He predicted that the Second Temple would be destroyed. In the last week of His life, Jesus pronounced judgment upon the Temple. We read.

> Jesus left the temple and was walking away when his disciples came up to him to call his attention to its buildings. "Do you see all these things?" he asked. "Truly I tell you, not one stone here will be left on another; every one will be thrown down" (Matthew 24:1-2 NIV).

According to Jesus, there would not be one stone left upon another when the Temple would be destroyed. Jesus also predicted the destruction of the city of Jerusalem. Luke records Him saying.

> The days will come upon you when your enemies will build an embankment against you and encircle you and hem you in on every side. They will dash you to the ground, you and the children within your walls. They will not leave one stone on another, because you did not recognize the time of God's coming to you. . . When you see Jerusalem being surrounded by armies, you will know that its desolation is near. Then let those who are in Judea flee to the mountains, let those in the

city get out, and let those in the country not enter the city (Luke 19:43,44; 21:20,21 NIV).

According to Jesus, the city of Jerusalem was to be sieged and the Temple destroyed.

GENTILE DOMINATION OF THE LAND AND ANOTHER EXILE ARE PREDICTED

Jesus also predicted that Jerusalem would be under Gentile domination and the people would be sent into another exile.

> They will fall by the edge of the sword and be led captive among all nations, and Jerusalem will be trampled underfoot by the Gentiles, until the times of the Gentiles are fulfilled (Luke 21:24 ESV).

The Jewish people would be sent away from their Holy Land. Gentiles would now rule the Promised Land instead of the Jews.

THERE IS A PREDICTED RETURN OF JESUS

Before He left this world, Jesus predicted that He would return. After Jesus' pronouncement of judgment upon the city of Jerusalem, the Jews, and the Temple, His disciples wanted to know what sign they could look for that would signal His return. The Bible records their questions.

> As Jesus was sitting on the Mount of Olives, the disciples came to him privately. "Tell us," they said, "when will this happen, and what will be the sign of your coming and of the end of the age?" (Matthew 24:3 NIV).

Jesus was asked about *the* sign which would signal His return.

JESUS GAVE A SPECIFIC SIGN: THE ABOMINATION OF DESOLATION

Jesus gave His disciples a specific sign to look for with regard to His return. Matthew records Him saying.

> So when you see standing in the holy place 'the abomi-
> nation that causes desolation,' spoken of through the
> prophet Daniel—let the reader understand . . . For then
> there will be great distress, unequaled from the beginning
> of the world until now—and never to be equaled again
> (Matthew 24:15,21 NIV).

Jesus said a time of "great distress" or "great tribulation" would occur before His return. The specific event, that would start this great tribulation, would be the "abomination of desolation." The abomination of desolation speaks of someone forcing the Temple sacrifices to cease, and defiling the holiness of the Temple. This is *the* future sign the people were to look for to know that His return is near. His Second Coming would occur soon after this event.

THERE WERE FALSE ACCUSATIONS ABOUT JESUS AND THE TEMPLE

The religious leaders arrested Jesus. One of the charges leveled at Him during His trial was that Christ said He would destroy the Temple. We read.

> But they did not find any, though many false witnesses came
> forward. Finally two came forward and declared, "This fel-
> low said, 'I am able to destroy the temple of God and rebuild
> it in three days'" (Matthew 26:60,61 NIV).

This accusation was based upon an earlier statement made by Jesus. John records the following incident.

> The Jews then responded to him, "What sign can you show
> us to prove your authority to do all this?" Jesus answered
> them, "Destroy this temple, and I will raise it again in three
> days." They replied, "It has taken forty-six years to build this
> temple, and you are going to raise it in three days?" But the
> temple he had spoken of was his body. After he was raised
> from the dead, his disciples recalled what he had said. Then

they believed the scripture and the words that Jesus had spoken (John 2:18-22 NIV).

The Temple that Jesus was referring was not the physical building, but rather His body that would be raised from the dead.

THE VEIL OF THE TEMPLE IS MIRACULOUSLY TORN

No evidence was brought forth that Jesus had done anything wrong. Nevertheless, He was sentenced to death. Matthew records that when Jesus died upon the cross, the veil of the Temple was torn.

> At that moment the curtain of the temple was torn in two from top to bottom. The earth shook, the rocks split (Matthew 27:51 NIV).

The Temple, which spoke of Jesus and His ministry, gave testimony in His death that He was the Promised Messiah!

The tearing of the veil signified that humanity now has direct access to God without going through a human priest. The New Testament declares.

> For there is one God and one intermediary between God and humanity, Christ Jesus, himself human (1 Timothy 2:5 NET).

Humanity now had direct access to God through the Person of Jesus Christ.

THE MESSIAH IS RISEN!

The New Testament records that Jesus Christ did not remain dead. As He predicted, He rose from the dead three days later. Forty days after His resurrection, Jesus ascended into heaven after reiterating His promise to come again. The Second Coming of Christ has been the hope of Christians for the last two thousand years.

THERE ARE OTHER TEMPLE REFERENCES IN THE NEW TESTAMENT

The references to the Temple in the remainder of the New Testament are few. The Apostle Paul, when speaking in Athens, emphasized that God is not limited to a physical building.

> And he is not served by human hands, as if he needed anything. Rather, he himself gives everyone life and breath and everything else. From one man he made all the nations, that they should inhabit the whole earth; and he marked out their appointed times in history and the boundaries of their lands (Acts 17:25-26 NIV).

The emphasis in the New Testament is on the New Covenant with the personal presence of Jesus the Messiah dwelling within each individual believer. He is in the midst of His people wherever they go, and whenever they gather in His name.

THE TEMPLE AND THE BELIEVERS BODY

Paul compared the Temple to the believer's body. He wrote the following.

> Don't you know that you yourselves are God's temple and that God's Spirit dwells in your midst? If anyone destroys God's temple, God will destroy that person; for God's temple is sacred, and you together are that temple (1 Corinthians 3:16-17 NIV).

In another place he wrote.

> Do you not know that your bodies are temples of the Holy Spirit, who is in you, whom you have received from God? You are not your own; you were bought at a price. Therefore honor God with your bodies (1 Corinthians 6:19,20 NIV).

The Apostle Peter compared the New Testament believers (the church) to a Temple. He put it this way.

So as you come to him, a living stone rejected by men but chosen and priceless in God's sight, you yourselves, as living stones, are built up as a spiritual house to be a holy priesthood and to offer a spiritual sacrifices that are acceptable to God through Jesus Christ (1 Peter 2:4-5 NET).

We are a spiritual temple. As such, we should conduct our lives in holiness to the Lord.

THE ATTEMPTED DESECRATION OF THE TEMPLE

Soon after the death and resurrection of Jesus, we have an episode involving the crazed Emperor Caligula and the attempted desecration of the Temple in Jerusalem.

The Roman Emperor Gaius Julius Caesar Germanicus, nicknamed Caligula ("little boots") began his reign with moderation, but soon was attacked by a disorder that seems to have left him a madman or a man possessed. He first declared himself "The One Master, the One King;" then he took the name of Pagan deities. Caligula ordered a temple built in his honor, and in it was placed a golden statue of himself. He appointed for his own worship a group of priests.

THERE WAS IDOLATRY IN ISRAEL

At this same time, some non-Jews brought idolatry into Israel. In the first century A.D., many pagans settled in the Judean city of Jamneh. These settlers desired to worship their heathen idols. The Jews would not tolerate any such pagan images in their city. When the idolatrous citizens of Jamneh learned that Caligula believed himself to be a god, they built an altar to him in their city.

The Jews immediately destroyed this idolatrous object. When the crazed Emperor heard about this destruction, he was incensed. Caligula ordered Petronius, the legate of Syria, to build a gigantic statue of himself, and to place it in the Holy of Holies in Jerusalem.

The sacrifices would no longer go to the God of Israel, but rather to Emperor Caligula. Instead of worshipping a God who was unseen, and who did not allow idols made of Him, the Jews would be commanded to worship the image of the Roman Emperor.

Flavius Josephus wrote of the incident.

> Now Caius Caesar did so grossly abuse the fortune he had arrived at, as to take himself to be a god, and to desire to be so called also, and to cut off those of the greatest nobility out of his country. He also extended his impiety as far as the Jews. Accordingly he sent Petronius with an army to Jerusalem to place his statues in the temple, and commanded him that, in case the Jews would not admit of them, he should slay those that opposed it, and carry all the rest into captivity.[1]

THIS WOULD HAVE FULFILLED JESUS' WORDS ABOUT THE SIGN OF THE END

Caligula's attempted act of abomination was similar to Antiochus' desecrating the Temple in 167 B.C. According to Jesus, that act of desecrating the Temple would be *the* sign that triggered the period He termed the "great tribulation," which would culminate in His Second Coming.

However, the time of His coming was not to be according to the whim of a Roman Emperor—rather it was to be in the times and seasons of His choice. The account of how this abomination was stopped is indeed fascinating.

AN IMAGE OF CALIGULA IS COMMISSIONED

The legate Petronius knew that the Jews would not permit an image to be placed in the Holy of Holies. Though he commissioned sculptors to carve the image, he made certain they went slowly.

---

1. Flavius Josephus, *Antiquities*, 2:20

Furthermore, Petronius was met by some 10,000 Jews in Tiberius. They told him they were all willing to die before they saw their Temple profaned. When the citizens of Judea discovered that an image was to be put in the Holy of Holies they told Petronius they would rather be killed than see the Holy of Holies violated. Petronius said he could not refuse the order of his Emperor. The Jews insisted they must obey the command of God.

SOME JEWS PLEAD WITH CALIGULA

At the same time, a group of Jews met with Caligula and pleaded that he not profane their Temple. Caligula said to them, "Oh! you are come, you enemies to the gods, who alone refuse to acknowledge me a god, while every other nation of the earth adores and worships me; but you reserve your worship for a God whose name you do not know"—at the same time stretching out his arm towards heaven, he uttered unspeakable blasphemies. He said of the Jews, "I think these people less wicked than mad and miserable, not to acknowledge my divinity."

THE ABOMINATION WAS AVERTED

The Jews were willing to sacrifice their entire nation before they would allow the Temple to be defiled. Petronius marveled at their courage and ceased with the process. Thus the confrontation was temporarily averted.

An enraged Caligula commanded that Petronius be put to death. Josephus records that Caligula died soon thereafter and due to bad weather at sea, the letter ordering Petronius' death arrived three weeks *after* the news arrived of Caligula's death. Petronius was not executed, and the Temple was spared this abomination. The time of the Messiah's return was not yet.

SUMMARY TO CHAPTER 8

The New Testament records that the Messiah came as promised. The people however rejected Him. Jesus then pronounced judgment upon the Jews, Jerusalem, and the Temple. Jesus predicted that He would someday return. Christ told His disciples to look for a specific sign that would precede His coming back—the abomination of desolation. This would take place in the Temple.

Shortly after Jesus' ascension, the mad Emperor Caligula ordered a giant statute of himself placed in the Jewish Temple. Had this happened, as he commanded, it would have fulfilled Jesus prediction of Matthew 24:15 regarding the abomination of desolation. This would have signaled Jesus' soon return.

But the time was not right for that to happen, and Caligula's plans were never carried out. The timing for the abomination of desolation was still future. It would not happen in the Second Temple, but will occur in a Third Temple—one that is still to be built.

CHAPTER 9

The Second Temple Is Destroyed: Another Jewish Exile Begins

They will fall by the sword and will be taken as prisoners to all the nations. Jerusalem will be trampled on by the Gentiles until the times of the Gentiles are fulfilled.

Jesus (Luke 21:24)

Before His death and resurrection, Jesus predicted that the Second Temple would be destroyed with not one stone standing upon another. He also predicted the fall of Jerusalem and that the people would be led away captive to other nations. Jesus further said that Jerusalem would fall under Gentile domination. All of these things He predicted have literally come to pass.

ENLARGEMENTS OF THE TEMPLE WERE FINALLY COMPLETED

As we mentioned, Herod started the work of rebuilding the Temple and enlarging the Temple Mount in 20-18 B.C. The Temple was then dedicated in 10 B.C. The work, however, was not finished.

First century Jewish historian, Flavius Josephus, wrote that the completion of the Second Temple did not occur until A.D. 63. Josephus tells us that 18,000 builders were still working at that time when they were finally dismissed.

Some thirty years previously, the Jews told Jesus that it had taken forty-six years to build the Temple (John 2:19). This probably meant that the workers had already been forty-six years at their task. The final result was an unbelievably beautiful structure. Unfortunately, it would not last very long.

THE JEWISH REVOLT

Because of heavy taxation by the Romans, the Jews staged a revolt in A.D. 66. The Roman garrison stationed in Jerusalem was massacred by the Jews. Rome reacted in anger. The governor of Syria led his army to Jerusalem to quiet the revolt but his soldiers were no match for the sheer number of Jews.

It would be several years before the problem would be settled. In A.D. 70, the Roman General Vespasian was sent to stop the Jewish uprising. Upon the death of Caesar Nero, he was called back to Rome to become Emperor. His son Titus was given the job of taking the city of Jerusalem.

THE SIEGE OF JERUSALEM

With four Legions, Titus began the siege of Jerusalem in April, A.D. 70. He posted his 10th legion on the Mount of Olives, directly east of and overlooking the Temple Mount. The 12th and 15th legions were stationed on Mount Scopus, further to the east, and commanding all ways to Jerusalem from east to north. The 5th legion was held in reserve.

During the siege, the Romans allowed anyone who wished to escape the city. Jewish believers in Jesus, remembering His prophecy regarding the destruction of Jerusalem and the Temple, fled the city to a place called Pella.

THE FATE OF THE TEMPLE DECIDED

Titus conferred with his fellow officers as to whether he should destroy the Temple along with the city. He thought that it would not be a good idea to destroy a structure so magnificent. Roman historian Tacitus reported what was discussed.

> The Roman commanders, led by Titus, conferred on the Mount of Olives on the eve of the fall of Jerusalem. The main item on the agenda was a question, the answer to which would have been self-understood in a campaign in any other part of the world: Should they destroy the Temple or not? It was accepted Roman policy to destroy all sources of power, including spiritual, of a rebellious province, and in this case the Temple was the focus of both temporal and spiritual Jewish independence. Titus, however, felt that it would not be wise to devastate this architectural gem—after all, the Romans were not barbarians!—and, after a bitter discussion, his opinion carried the day.

> The principal officers were of the opinion that nothing less than the utter destruction of the Temple would secure a lasting peace. A building, which the Jews themselves had made a theatre of blood, ought not, they contended, to be any longer considered a place of worship. It was rather a citadel in which the garrison remained in force . . . and ought to be given up to the fury of an enraged soldiery.[1]

Though Titus ordered the Temple to be spared, One greater than Titus had already spoken! When the city was destroyed the stones of the Temple were pulled down in exact accordance with the words of Jesus.

THE CITY AND TEMPLE ARE DESTROYED

On the 10th of August, in A.D. 70, the 9th of Av in Jewish reckoning, the very day when Nebuchadnezzar burned the Temple in 587 B.C., the Temple was burned again. Titus took the city and put it to the torch.

---

1. Tacitus, *Historiae*, 5, 9:1

Jewish historian, Flavius Josephus was present in Jerusalem when the city was captured, and the Temple was burnt. He described the event in this manner.

> The Romans, though it was a terrible struggle to collect the timber, raised their platforms in twenty-one days, having, as described before, stripped the whole area in a circle round the town to a distance of ten miles. The countryside like the City was a pitiful sight; for where once there had been a lovely vista of woods and parks there was nothing but desert and stumps of trees. No one—not even a foreigner—who had seen the Old Judea and the glorious suburbs of the City, and now set eyes on her present desolation, could have helped sighing and groaning at so terrible a change; for every trace of beauty had been blotted out by war, and nobody who had known it in the past and came upon it suddenly would have recognized the place: when he was already there he would still have been looking for the City.[2]

THE OUTCOME OF THE SIEGE

Josephus detailed the horrendous outcome.

> To give a detailed account of their outrageous conduct is impossible, but we may sum it up by saying that no other city has ever endured such horrors, and no generation in history has fathered such wickedness. In the end they brought the whole Hebrew race into contempt in order to make their own impiety seem less outrageous in foreign eyes, and confessed the painful truth that they were slaves, the dregs of humanity, bastards, and outcasts of their nation. It is certain that when from the upper city they watched the Temple burning they did not turn a hair, though many Romans were moved to tears.[3]

---

2. Flavius Josephus, *Wars of the Jews*, Book 5.4:2
3. Flavius Josephus, *Wars of the Jews*, Book 5.4:4

Though Titus had ordered the Temple to be spared, an excited Roman soldier threw a torch into it, causing it to be burned.

Josephus gave eyewitness testimony to the last moments of the Temple.

> As the flames shot into the air the Jews sent up a cry that matched the calamity and dashed to the rescue, with no thought now of saving their lives or husbanding their strength; for that which hitherto they had guarded so devotedly was disappearing before their eyes.[4]

THE TEMPLE VESSELS ARE TAKEN

The conquering Titus took the Temple vessels with him to Rome. Josephus wrote.

> Titus removed the veil (which separated between the Holy and the Holy of Holies) and spread it out like a net. He gathered all the sacred Temple vessels together and placed them inside, and then embarked by ship for Rome, to boast and to seek honor.[5]

THE PREDICTION OF JESUS IS LITERALLY FULFILLED

The predictions of Jesus, with respect to the city and the Temple, were now fulfilled. The disciples could not possibly have understood the Lord to mean anything but the literal Jerusalem when He uttered the prediction about its destruction.

Indeed, there is no controversy with regard to the literal fulfillment of this prophecy. Jerusalem was literally destroyed, and the stones from which its magnificent Temple was built, were literally thrown down.

---

4. Flavius Josephus, *Wars of the Jews*, Book 5.10:5
5. Flavius Josephus, *Wars of the Jews*, Book 6.5:1

THE TEMPLE IS DESTROYED AFTER THE MESSIAH HAD COME

As the prophet Daniel had predicted, the Temple was destroyed after the Messiah had come. We read.

> After the sixty-two 'sevens,' the Anointed One will be put to death and will have nothing. The people of the ruler who will come will destroy the city and the sanctuary (Daniel 9:26 NIV).

Jesus stated the reason—they did not recognize the coming of the Messiah. In fact, Jesus said this while He cried over Jerusalem on Palm Sunday.

> As he approached Jerusalem and saw the city, he wept over it and said, "If you, even you, had only known on this day what would bring you peace—but now it is hidden from your eyes. The days will come upon you when your enemies will build an embankment against you and encircle you and hem you in on every side. They will dash you to the ground, you and the children within your walls. They will not leave one stone on another, because you did not recognize the time of God's coming to you" (Luke 19:41-44 NIV).

The Word of God was again fulfilled.

THE ABOMINATION OF DESOLATION DID NOT OCCUR AT THAT TIME

The Second Temple was destroyed without fulfilling the words of Jesus regarding the Abomination of Desolation. There was no stopping of the sacrifices, or defiling of the Holy of Holies as this prophecy called for. Indeed, the sign of the Abomination of Desolation was given by Jesus to signal His immediate return. He did not return in A.D. 70 when the Temple was destroyed. The fulfillment will occur in the future when a Third Temple is built, and the sacrifices are restored.

THERE WAS A SECOND FORCED EXILE OF THE PEOPLE

When the Temple was destroyed in A.D. 70, the period of the Second Exile began. The Jewish people were scattered throughout the earth. In fact, for the next 1,900 years the Jews would have no authority in the land that God had promised them.

SUMMARY TO CHAPTER 9

The predictions of Jesus were all literally fulfilled. The city of Jerusalem was taken by the Gentiles (Romans), the Temple was destroyed, and the people were sent into exile. These were God's punishments for not receiving Jesus as their promised Messiah. The destruction of the Temple in A.D. 70, and the exile of the Jews, began a long, sad chapter in their history in which they would experience unimaginable suffering. This fulfilled the words spoken by Jesus on His way to the cross.

> Jesus turned and said to them, "Daughters of Jerusalem, do not weep for me; weep for yourselves and for your children. For the time will come when you will say, 'Blessed are the childless women, the wombs that never bore and the breasts that never nursed!' Then they will say to the mountains, "Fall on us!" and to the hills, "Cover us!" (Luke 23:28-30 NIV).

This weeping would continue for a long time.

CHAPTER 10

The Temple Mount in Ruin: Futile Attempts are Made to Rebuild

Because of our sins we were exiled from our country and banished from our land. We cannot go up as pilgrims to worship You, to perform our duties in Your chosen house, the great and Holy Temple which was called by Your name, on account of the hand that was let loose on Your sanctuary. May it be Your will, Lord our God and God of our fathers, merciful King, in Your abundant love again to have mercy on us and on Your sanctuary; rebuild it speedily and magnify its glory.

Traditional Jewish prayer book

Although most of the Jewish nation was in exile from their land, the Jews did not forget Jerusalem or the Temple Mount. Their daily prayer was for the rebuilding of the Temple in Jerusalem. They also testified that the world needed the Temple.

If the nations of the world had only known how much they needed the Temple, they would have surrounded it with armed fortresses to protect it.

In the first few centuries after the destruction of the Second Temple, there were some attempts by the Jews to rebuild their destroyed sanctuary. All of these attempts ended in failure.

THE FIRST ATTEMPT TO REBUILD THE TEMPLE

In the first hundred years after Jerusalem and the Temple were destroyed, there was high expectation among the Jews that they would once again return to their land, and rebuild the city and the Temple. The Court of Seventy Elders, the Sanhedrin, was intact and many Jews still lived in small communities in Israel. Attempts were made during this time to have a Third Temple built.

THE TIME OF HADRIAN

The first recorded instance of an attempt to rebuild the Temple occurred in the reign of Hadrian (A.D. 118-135)—a few years after the Second Temple was destroyed.

Though the information is not clear, there is some evidence that Hadrian gave the Jews permission to rebuild their Temple early in his reign. The Jewish Encyclopedia writes.

> It appears that Hadrian already granted permission for the rebuilding of the Temple; that the Jews of the Diaspora had already begun to return to Jerusalem, and that the brothers Pappus and Julian had already provided for the exchange of foreign money into Roman coin.[1]

Hadrian seems to have requested that the site of the new Temple be different from its former location. This was, of course, unsatisfactory to the Jews as Rabbi Chaim Richman notes.

> In the time of Rabbi Yehoshua Ben Chananya, the evil empire decreed that the Temple may be rebuilt. Two wealthy Jews, Papus and Lulianus were appointed to finance the project. They accompanied the exiles along the way from Acre until Antioch, supplied them with silver, gold and all their needs.

---

1. *Jewish Encyclopedia*, Volume 1, p. 213

Meanwhile the Samaritans went to the Emperor and lied. They said: 'Know, O King, that the Jews are rebelling against you! When they rebuild the Temple, they will cease to pay the royal taxes.' Hadrian replied, 'What should I do? I already authorized the decree!'

They responded: 'All you need to do is send a message to them saying, 'Change the location of the Temple just a bit— or, add on another five cubits to the site.' Then they will withdraw of their own accord.'

The whole nation had gathered in the valley of Beit Rimon when the Emperor's edict arrived. They began to wail and cry. They considered rebelling against Hadrian, but Rabbi Yehoshua Ben Chananya rose and spoke before them. 'It is enough that we have escaped from these people with our lives,' he said. The Jews dispersed and each man returned to his home.[2]

Whether the rebuilding process was actually started during the early years of Hadrian's reign is uncertain.

THE SECOND JEWISH REVOLT

The Jews rebelled against the Romans in what is known as the "Second Jewish Revolt." Rome responded with large scale mass murders of Jews in Caesarea and other communities. The murders sparked a larger rebellion—led by a man named Bar Kochba in A.D. 132. Bar Kochba rallied the people and massacred the famous 12th legion of the Roman army. Jerusalem was liberated for three years. Rabbi Akiva proclaimed Bar Kochba as the Messiah—the one who was to deliver the Jewish people.

---

2. Chaim Richman, *The Odyssey Of The Third Temple*, Israel Publications And Productions, n.d., p. 68

The Jews set up an independent government. Coins were struck that commemorated the "First Year of the Deliverance of Israel." Another coin that was struck showed the facade of the Temple.

Within three years of Jerusalem's liberation, Rome marched against the rebels and killed Bar Kochba. The Sanhedrin labeled him a false Messiah, and Jerusalem was again in Roman hands.

WAS THERE ANOTHER REBUILDING ATTEMPT?

It is probable that attempts were made to rebuild the Temple during the period of A.D. 132-135. One later historical work describes Hadrian as the one who destroyed the Temple of the Jews. The Roman historian, Dio Cassius, also said that Hadrian built his Temple to replace the one of the God of Israel.

Some, therefore, assume that these references are not referring to the destruction of the original Temple by Titus in A.D. 70, but to a later destruction by Hadrian of a partially restored Temple built by Bar Kochba. Of this, however, we cannot be certain. Rabbi Chaim Richman notes.

> Owing to the inaccuracies in the reporting of the rebellion's progress found in both Roman testimonies and traditional Jewish sources, it remains unclear whether or not the fighters achieved their objective of even temporarily renewing the Temple service.[3]

A NEW NAME FOR JERUSALEM

Jewish Jerusalem was blotted out. The city was plowed under and then rebuilt with a new name—*Aelia Capitolina*. Because the war had cost the lives of Roman heroes, the Jews were forbidden to enter Jerusalem

---

3. Chaim Richman, *The Odyssey Of The Third Temple*, Israel Publications And Productions, n.d., p. 71

upon penalty of death. Hadrian attempted to destroy every connection Jerusalem had with the Jewish people.

In an effort to leave no trace of the Temple, Hadrian built a Temple to Jupiter Capitolinus on the Temple Mount. An equestrian statue of Hadrian was also built in front of it. A small temple to Venus was also built (the present site of the church of the Holy Sepulcher).

The next Emperor, Antonius Pius (A.D. 138-161), added another statue. The Jews were only allowed to enter the city on special occasions to mourn on the Temple Mount.

JERUSALEM'S NAME RESTORED

In the fourth century, the Roman Emperor Constantine and his mother Queen Helen were converted to Christianity. In A.D. 324, Aelia Capitolina was renamed Jerusalem and the title of "Holy City" was restored to her. It was now, however, considered the Holy City of Christianity. The pagan temple of Jupiter was destroyed, and the church of Holy Zion was built upon the Temple Mount. These conditions lasted until A.D. 362 when the Roman emperor Julian the Apostate permitted the Jews to return.

THE TEMPLE WAS TO BE REBUILT

In the early years of the church, it was still believed by Christians that the Jews would come back to their land, and rebuild their Temple. This rebuilding would be in unbelief of Jesus. Many of the early Christian commentators, who took the Bible literally, assumed this would happen. God, they believed, was not finished with the nation Israel. It was only a matter of time when the predicted events were fulfilled.

For example, Irenaeus (140-202) wrote that the coming Antichrist would sit in a rebuilt Jerusalem Temple.

> He will reign a time, times, and half a time (Daniel 7:25) i.e. three and a half years and will sit in the temple at Jerusalem;

then the Lord shall come from heaven and cast him into the lake of fire, and shall bring to the saints the time of reigning, the seventh day of hallowed rest, and give to Abraham the promised inheritance.[4]

THERE WAS A CHANGE IN THE CHRISTIAN PERSPECTIVE

However, a change began to occur among Christians as to their perspective of Jerusalem, and the Temple. Jerusalem began to be seen as the spiritual center for the *church*. The holy places of the Jews were replaced with the holy places of the Christians. The Temple Mount lay in neglect. As long as the Temple Mount was in ruins, the church saw this as Christianity triumphing over Judaism. The church considered itself the "New Jerusalem."

REPLACEMENT THEOLOGY

The idea that the church was the New Jerusalem caused many interpreters to take the Old Testament promises to the Jews, and to replace them with promises to the church. No longer was it believed that God had a plan for the Jewish people. When the Jews rejected Jesus, it was contended that God rejected them.

Furthermore, a continuing sign that God had cursed the Jews was the destruction of the Temple, and the ruined condition of the Temple Mount. The Jews, Jerusalem, and the Temple were no longer in the plan of God according to "replacement theology."

THE SPIRITUALIZATION OF PROPHECY

Biblical prophecy began to be spiritualized. Therefore, there was to be no literal fulfillment of the promises to Abraham descendants. These promises were now to be fulfilled in the new people of God— the church. The truth of the Christian faith, according to some early

---

4. Irenaeus, *Against Heresies*, Book V, Chapter 30, paragraph 4

Christians, now depended upon the Temple in Jerusalem remaining in ruins—never to be rebuilt. A rebuilt Temple, they erroneously supposed, would contradict the words of Jesus about its destruction.

THE MOUNT WAS CURSED OF GOD

As Christianity gained foothold in the Roman world, the Temple Mount was left to become a desolate rubble heap. Jewish writers Meir Ben-Dov, Mordechai Naor and Zeev Aner note.

> When Christianity became the official religion of the Roman Empire at the beginning of the fourth century, maintaining Jerusalem and the Temple in ruins because an important policy of its emperors. Emperor Constantine and his successors saw the destruction of the Temple as a symbol of Judaism's demise and growth of Christianity in its place. They therefore strictly enforced Hadrian's edicts; Jews were not allowed to settle in the city and, above all, the Temple Mount was to remain devastated as a memorial to the liquidation of Judaism in its previous form. Only on the ninth of Av were the Jews allowed into Jerusalem to bewail the destruction of the Temple. We can assume that on that day Christian propagandists mingled with the mourners to preach their explanation of the Temple's destruction and what it signified.[5]

In A.D. 534, over the site of Solomon's elaborate palace, the Emperor Justinian built mighty substructures as foundations for the New Church of St. Mary. While other holy sites in Jerusalem were explored and identified, the Temple Mount was still neglected.

THE MADABA MAP

A map that was constructed in the sixth century, known as the Madaba map, provided the contemporary feeling of the Christians towards

---

5. Meir Ben-Dov, Mordechai Naor, Zeev Aner, *The Western Wall*, Jerusalem, Ministry of Defense Publishing House, 1983, p. 5

Jerusalem and the Temple Mount. The city of Jerusalem is outlined in the map, with the Temple Mount noticeably missing. It was as though the area did not exist!

To the Christians living at that time, the destroyed Temple and the ruined Temple Mount, testified to the superiority of Christianity over Judaism. Jesus' prophecy of the destroyed Temple had been fulfilled and the site was left in ruin as a testimony to His prediction.

THE TEMPLE—THE PLACE OF DUNG

Not only was the Temple Mount deliberately left in ruin, further insult was added. In the seventh century the Temple Mount was made a dumping place for dung. Today one approaches the Temple Mount from the Dung Gate—the name derived from this time when the dung was left on the Mount.

By making the Temple Mount a place for their excrement, the "Christians" were emphasizing God's judgment upon this site.

THE SAME IDEA IS FOUND IN MODERN TIMES

Lest we think that only those in the Byzantine times considered the Temple Mount a place of dung, some in modern times have accepted the same terrible idea. The famous British General, Charles Gordon, arrived in Jerusalem in 1883, and identified a hill as the scene of Jesus' crucifixion—Mt. Calvary. *Calvary* is the Latin word for skull (*Golgotha* in Aramaic). Since Calvary, or Golgotha, was the place of the skull Gordon visualized a skeleton over the city of Jerusalem. The skull was aligned with Calvary.

However, the Temple Mount, in his skeleton, was considered the place of excrement in Gordon's visualization of the outline of Jerusalem. Hence, the idea continued that the place of the First and Second Jewish Temple should be viewed as a place of human waste.

THE REMAINS OF THE TEMPLE WERE STILL VISIBLE

Though the Temple Mount lay in ruins after the destruction of the Temple, we have some information from ancient sources concerning visible remains of the Temple in the years after it was leveled to the ground.

Eusebius, bishop of Caesarea (A.D. 260-340), testified that he could still see the remains of the sanctuary. He said that the large stone blocks were hauled away to build sanctuaries and theaters.

THE PILGRIM OF BORDEAUX

During this period of Exile, the city was visited by a pilgrim known as the traveler of Bordeaux (France). He gave the following testimony in A.D. 333.

> At the side of the Sanctuary, there is a pierced stone. Jews visit there once a year, pour oil over it, lament and weep over it, and tear their garments in token of mourning. Then they return home.

> The once a year visit was on the 9th of Av, the Jewish date of the destruction of both Temples. The pierced stone, or a rock with a hollow in it, is not identified. It is assumed to be the foundation stone upon which the Holy of Holies was built, although some take this expression to mean the Western Wall. In the Talmud we find a reference to the "Foundation Rock" upon which the Holy of Holies had rested (Yoma 5:2).

EARLY CHRISTIAN TESTIMONY TO THE TEMPLE MOUNT

Early church father John Chrysostom wrote about the conditions in the city of Jerusalem in the fourth century.

> The Jews began uncovering the foundations by removing masses of earth, intending to go ahead and build . . . You can

see the bared foundations if you visit Jerusalem now. . . Some of its parts (the sanctuary) are razed to the ground.

In A.D. 392, the Christian leader Jerome wrote about the Jew's practice on the anniversary of the Temple's destruction.

> On the anniversary of the day when the city fell and was destroyed by the Romans, there are crowds who mourn, old women and old men dressed in tatters and rags, and from the top of the Mount of Olives this throng laments over the destruction of its Sanctuary. Still their eyes flow with tears, still their hands tremble and their hair is disheveled, but already the guards demand pay for their right to weep.[6]

In the sixth century, the Pilgrim of Piacenze mentioned the ruins of the Temple of Solomon on his visit to Jerusalem.

From these accounts we can deduce that there were at least some visible remains of the Temple through the sixth century.

JULIAN THE ANTI-CHRISTIAN EMPEROR

There was only one other occasion, since the destruction of the Second Temple, that serious plans were made to rebuild. The person behind this project was the Roman Emperor, Flavius Claudius Julianus, a nephew of Constantine.

> The Emperor Julian, known as Julian the Apostate, determined that he would rebuild the Temple and so disprove the words of Jesus. But the attempt, like all other efforts to discredit the Word of God, resulted in a testimony of the truth of the prophetic Scriptures.[7]

---

6. Jerome, Commentary on Isaiah 2:9
7. L. Peres Buroker, *Yesterday in Bible Prophecy*, Lapeer, Michigan, 1938, p. 24

Julian planned the project in the last year of his reign in A.D. 363. He rescinded all the anti-Jewish laws that his uncle Constantine had instituted. He issued an edict that the Temple be rebuilt in Jerusalem.

This caused a great deal of excitement among the Jews. From far and wide, Jews came to Jerusalem to help in the rebuilding work. Julian supplied the necessary funds and appointed Alypius of Antioch, Governor of Great Britain, to carry out the project. Jews from all over gave from their wealth upon the projected work of rebuilding the Temple. The roads to Jerusalem were filled with multitudes of Jewish men and women who had hopes of seeing a Third Temple built.

Edward Gibbon, in his *Decline and Fall of the Roman Empire*, described the scene.

> The men forgot their avarice, and the women their delicacy; spades and pickaxes of silver were provided by the vanity of the rich, and the rubbish was transported in mantle of silk and purple.

The Mysterious Destruction

However, tragedy struck. The foundations were barely uncovered when flames of fire burst forth from under the ground. The flames were accompanied by large explosions.

The workmen fled and the building was stopped—never again to be restarted. A massive earthquake had struck Jerusalem. Philip Hammond explains what happened.

> The stones were piled and ready. Costly wood had been purchased. The necessary metal was at hand. The Jews of Jerusalem were rejoicing. Tomorrow—May 20, 363 A.D.– the rebuilding of the Temple would begin! Almost 300 years after the Roman Legions under Titus had destroyed the Temple, the Emperor Julian—called by his Christian

subjects "the Apostate"—had given his imperial permission to rebuild the Temple. The Jewish people eagerly responded. . . Suddenly, and without warning, at the third hour of the night (the third hour after sunset according to Roman practice) the streets of Jerusalem trembled and buckled, crushing three hundred years of hope in a pile of dust. No longer would there be any possibility of rebuilding the Temple.[8]

Gibbon, who had no love for Christianity or the Bible, explained what happened.

> An earthquake, a whirlwind, and a fiery eruption which overturned and scattered the new foundations of the Temple, are attested with some variations, by contemporary and respectable evidence.

Quoting Ammaianus Marcellinus, Gibbon writes.

> Whilst Alypius, assisted by the governor of the province, urged with vigor and diligence the execution of the work, horrible balls of fire breaking out near the foundations, with frequent and reiterated attacks, rendered the place from time to time, inaccessible to the scorched and blasted workmen; and the victorious element continuing in this manner obstinately and resolutely bent, as it were, to drive them to a distance, the undertaking was abandoned.

Many explanations have been offered of the strange phenomena which halted the building operations. Among other things, it has been suggested that the caverns and underground passages which underlay the Temple area were filled with gas which became ignited. But whatever the explanation, the significant fact remains that a deliberate attempt was made to set aside the prophecy and that attempt was without success.

---

8. Phillip Hammond, "New Light on the Nabateans," *Biblical Archaeology Review,* March/April, 1981, p. 21

THE WRATH OF GOD?

There are those who believed that the earthquake was a demonstration of the anger of God. With their hopes dashed, the Jews were then driven into exile, and became wanderers in foreign lands. They were people without a homeland. In fact, for some eighteen centuries they would be dispersed and persecuted. Throughout time, their thoughts were of the Temple that once stood in Jerusalem, and their prayers were for its restoration.

A PROMISE TO REBUILD THE TEMPLE

The control of Jerusalem switched hands when the Persians conquered the Byzantine Empire. The Jews in their fight against the Christians aided the Persians. In return for their help, the Persians promised the Jews national freedom and the permission to rebuild the Temple. But the rebuilding of the Temple would not come to pass on this occasion.

> In 614 Chosroes II, king of Persia, conquered . . . Israel, Syria and portions of Asia Minor from the Byzantines. He was helped by the Jews and in appreciation made them rulers of Jerusalem. The way was now open to restore the Temple Mount and rebuild the Temple. However, after only three years the Persian-Jewish alliance was abrogated because the Persians were afraid of the large Christian population of Jerusalem. Anyway the Persians held their conquests for only a short time; in 628 the Byzantine Christians reconquered everything from the Persians, including Jerusalem.[9]

Jewish hopes were again thwarted with regard to the rebuilding of the Temple. The time to build was still in the future.

---

9. Meir Ben-Dov, Mordechai Naor, Zeev Aner, *The Western Wall*, Jerusalem, Ministry of Defense Publishing House, 1983, p. 12

SUMMARY TO CHAPTER 10

In the centuries after its destruction the few attempts to rebuild the Temple failed. The desire was there but the circumstances would not permit it. The time was not yet right. The more that time passed the realization set in that the Temple would not be speedily rebuilt. The Christians, wishing to celebrate the triumph of Christianity over Judaism, left the Temple Mount in rubble. They saw the neglect of the Temple Mount as a testimony to the truth of Jesus' prophecy concerning the destruction of the Temple.

Furthermore, they began to spiritualize the literal prophecies of the Old Testament with respect to Abraham and his descendants. They saw no future for Israel in the plan of God—the church inherited the promises made to Abraham. Therefore, they were not looking for the Jews to return to their land and rebuild their Temple.

A new player was about to arrive on the scene that would change the face of Jerusalem and the Temple Mount—a change that would remain until the present day.

CHAPTER 11

The Temple Mount Becomes Important to a New Religion: Islam

Ten parts of beauty were allotted the world at large, and of
these Jerusalem assumed nine measures and the rest of the
world but one . . . ten parts of suffering were visited upon the
world—nine for Jerusalem and one for the world

The Jewish Sages

The rulership over Jerusalem was again to change hands. On this occasion, it would be by a new religion which exploded upon the world scene in the 7th Century A.D.—Islam. From a humble beginning, Islam would become a major world religion with millions of followers. The legacy of Islam would be far-reaching, for its control of the Temple Mount extends until this very day.

ISLAM AND JERUSALEM

Four years after the death of the Muhammad, the founder of Islam, an army of his followers surrounded Jerusalem. The city Patriarch Sophronius, handed over the city after a brief siege. British historian Steve Runciman relates the incident when an Islamic army conquered the holy city.

> On a February day in the year A.D. 638 the Caliph Omar
> entered Jerusalem, riding upon a white camel. He was
> dressed in worn, filthy robes, and the army that followed him

was rough and unkempt; but its discipline was perfect. At his side was the Patriarch Sophronius, as chief magistrate of the surrendered city. Omar rode straight to the site of the Temple of Solomon, whence his friend Mahomet had ascended into heaven. Watching him stand there, the Patriarch remembered the words of Christ and murmured through his tears: 'Behold the abomination of desolation, spoken of by Daniel the prophet'.[1]

Omar was shocked at the filth and rubble that lay strewn about. Because the holy site had been neglected, he made the Christian Patriarch Sophronius grovel in the muck. Afterward Omar set about clearing the site. A huge timber mosque, which held three thousand worshippers, was erected on this site in the time of Omar, at the southernmost wall of the Temple Mount.

THE DOME OF THE ROCK

In A.D. 691, Caliph Abd El-Malik commissioned the best architects to build a shrine commemorating Muhammad's alleged flight into heaven. This shrine became known as the "Dome of the Rock." It was built as a political, economic, and religious counter attraction to Mecca. Medina and Mecca, the two cities holy to Islam, were under the control of a rival Caliph. Abd El-Malik wanted to build up the importance of Jerusalem as an Islamic center for pilgrimage and worship. The holiest spot of the Jews, the site of their Temple, was now identified with the spot where Muhammad's horse ascended to heaven.

Although Abd El-Malik had commissioned the structure, it became known as "The Mosque of Omar." The structure, however, is not a mosque but rather a shrine.

---

1. Steve Runciman, *A History of the Crusades*, Volume One, "The First Crusade," Cambridge University Press, 1951, p. 3

IT HAS UNDERGONE CHANGES

During the thirteen centuries of the Dome's existence, it has undergone many repairs, but it has not been substantially changed since its completion in A.D. 691. After one of the earliest renovations in A.D. 820, Caliph al-Mamun took off the name of Caliph Abd el-Malik from the dedication plate, and inserted his own name instead. However, he neglected to change the dates. Therefore, his fraud is there for all the world to see.

In medieval times this particular spot was considered to be the "center of the world" and was marked as such on various maps.

WAS THE DOME BUILT OVER THE TEMPLE SITE?

Inside the Dome is the "Sacred Rock." The same rock is the traditional site of Abraham's sacrificial altar for Isaac, as well as the site of the First and Second Temple. It is generally assumed that the Dome was purposely built over the previous Temples to keep the Jews from ever constructing another Temple on the Temple Mount.

SACRED TRADITIONS ABOUT THE ROCK

The sacred rock has been the source of many traditions that have grown up over the centuries. Islamic tradition teaches that Allah went up to heaven from this spot after he created all things.

Muslims also maintain that this rock fell from heaven about the time that the spirit of prophecy was imparted. They also believe that this rock was also the first place from which the waters of the Flood receded. Muslim tradition has Allah saying, "This is my place and the place of my seat on the day of resurrection."

MUHAMMAD'S FLIGHT

It is taught that this holy stone wished to accompany the prophet Muhammad to heaven in his famous "night flight," but was restrained by the angel Gabriel. The angel Gabriel held the rock so firmly that the impression of his hand on the rock is still pointed out to this day.

On the south side of this rock the "footprint" of Muhammad is found. On his famous "Night Flight" where he supposedly ascended into the presence of Allah in the seventh heaven, he left his foot impression in the rock.

OTHER TRADITIONS

East of the rock is a tall cupboard where it is believed hairs from the beard of Muhammad are contained. Within the hollowed out chamber of the rock are the "places of prayer" of Elijah, Abraham, David, and Solomon. The Muslims call this cave the "well of souls" where they believe the dead meet twice a week to pray.

Muslims believe the Dome of the Rock contains God's scales for the weighing of the souls of men.

> The Mighty stretched out his hands toward the places that he wished to point out, saying: 'This to the west is the garden of Eden; This to the East is the fire of hell and this is the place of my scales of Justice.'

It is believed the sacred rock also contains the shield of their "prophet" Muhammad and the saddle of el-Burak-Lightning—the steed on which the prophet made his night flight from Mecca to Jerusalem. There is also an early copy of Islam's Holy Book, the Koran; of which the parchment leaves are four feet long.

Because of Muslim belief that all these events took place from this rock, the spot is housed by a shrine and held to be sacred. The sanctity and awe with which Muslims regard this spot is beyond description. The Crusaders were known to chip "holy souvenirs" from it.

THE DOME'S BEAUTY

Writing about A.D. 985, Mukadassi, the famous Muslim traveler born in Jerusalem, wrote.

> At the dawn, when the light of the sun first strikes on the cupola and the drum catches the rays, then is this edifice a marvelous site to behold and one such that in all Islam I have never seen its equal; neither have I heard tell of aught built in pagan times that could rival in grace this Dome of the Rock.

THE DENIAL OF CHRISTIANITY

From the Muslim point of view, the Dome of the Rock was an answer to, and a denial of, the attractions of Christianity and its Scriptures, providing the "faithful" with arguments to be used against Christian theology.

The inscriptions on its walls are seven hundred and thirty-four feet long in all, amongst the lengthiest inscriptions in the world. There is a great amount of repetition and many quotations from the Koran. The following extracts are relevant.

THE INNER FACE

South Wall: In the name of Allah the Merciful the Compassionate. There is no God but Allah alone; he has no co-partner. He is the Kingship and his is the praise. He gives life and he causes to die, and he has power over everything.

Southeast Wall: Truly Allah and his angels pronounce blessing upon the Prophet. O you who have pronounced blessings upon him and give Him the salutation of peace. O, People of the Book (i.e. the Jews and Christians always referred to as such by the Muslims) do not go beyond the bounds in your religion and do not say about Allah anything but the truth. The Messiah, Jesus, son of Mary, is but a messenger of Allah and his word, which he cast upon Mary, and a spirit from him. So believe only in Allah and of his messenger, but do not say "Three" (Trinity) and it will be better for you. Allah is only one God. Far be it from his glory that he should have a son.

Northwest Wall: The son of Mary and peace be upon him the day of his birth, the day of his death and the day of his being raised alive. That is Jesus, son of Mary—a statement concerning which YOU are in doubt. It is not for Allah to take for himself any offspring, glory be to him.

Southwest Wall: Upholding justice. There is no God but he, the Almighty and All wise. Verily, the religion in Allah's sight is Islam.

THE OUTER FACE

West and Northwest Walls: In the name of Allah the Merciful and Compassionate. There is no God but Allah alone. Praise be to Allah who has not taken to himself offspring. To him there has never been any person in the sovereignty. Muhammad is the messenger of Allah, may God pray upon him and accept his intercession. Praise be God who has not taken unto himself a son and who has no partner in sovereignty nor has He any protector on account of weakness.

THESE ARE BLASPHEMIES AGAINST JESUS CHRIST

An inspection of the sayings on the wall will reveal that they contain blasphemies against Jesus Christ. Emphasis is made that God would not have a Son. Islam blatantly denies the basic message of the gospel; the relationship of Jesus to His Father. The Bible makes it clear that Jesus was God the Son. We read.

> As soon as the chief priests and their officials saw him, they shouted, "Crucify! Crucify!" But Pilate answered, "You take him and crucify him. As for me, I find no basis for a charge against him." The Jewish leaders insisted, "We have a law, and according to that law he must die, because he claimed to be the Son of God" (John 19:6-7 NIV).

Islam denies this biblical truth.

THE AL AQSA MOSQUE

The Al-Aqsa Mosque (sometime spelled El Aqsa or Al Aksa) is located some 100 yards to the south of the Dome of the Rock. This Mosque is the third holiest site in all Islam, behind only Mecca and Medina. Hence, Muslims consider the entire Temple Mount area holy. Al Aqsa is supposedly mentioned in the Koran in a vision of Muhammad's ascension. It means the "distant place." The present mosque is believed to stand over the area where Solomon built his magnificent palace south of the Temple.

The Al Aqsa Mosque was built between A.D. 709-715 by Caliph Waleed, son of Abd el-Malik—the man who constructed the Dome of the Rock. Throughout the years the mosque has been destroyed several times by earthquakes, and subsequently rebuilt. A few supporting columns east of the cupola are the most prominent remains that have survived of the original mosque.

The most important reconstruction was after an earthquake in A.D. 1034. The mosque was then enlarged to seat 5000 worshipers. The builders used capitals and columns of destroyed Byzantine churches in their reconstruction.

ISLAM AND THE TEMPLE MOUNT

Since it is a historical fact that Muhammad never came to Jerusalem, why is the Temple Mount considered holy to Muslims? There is a passage from the Koran that supposedly links Muhammad with Jerusalem and the Temple Mount. It is in the seventeenth Sura, "The Night Journey." In it there is a dream, or vision, by Muhammad in which he is carried by night.

> From the sacred temple to the temple that is more remote, whose precinct we have blessed, that we might show him of our signs (Koran, Sura 17).

Islamic tradition identifies the first temple as Mecca and the second as Jerusalem. Muhammad's journey was with the Archangel Gabriel. Muslim belief says they rode together on a winged steed called El Burak ("lightning"). El Burak is not mentioned in the Koran; its first mention is two centuries after Muhammad's death in a document called the *Hadith*, a collection of oral traditions.

In sum, as it has always been for Jews, the Temple Mount has become a sacred place to Islam.

SUMMARY TO CHAPTER 11

Islam arrived on the scene in the seventh century. On the Temple Mount there was built a shrine (the Dome of the Rock) and a Mosque (Al Aqsa). The Dome of the Rock was likely built over what they believed was the site of the First and Second Temple. This, they assumed, would prevent the Jews from ever building a future Temple on the same spot. The control of the Temple Mount by Islam has remained to this day— as has the struggle between Jews, Muslims, and Christians.

CHAPTER 12

The Temple Mount Continues to be Defiled:
The Jews Remain in Forced Exile

> You will live in constant suspense, filled with dread both
> night and day, never sure of your life. In the morning you
> will say, "If only it were evening!" and in the evening, "If
> only it were morning!"—because of the terror that will fill
> your hearts and the sights that your eyes will see.
>
> Deuteronomy 28:66,67

The Old Testament warnings of God, and the New Testament words
of Jesus, the God-Man, continued to be fulfilled. The city of Jerusalem
was in the hands of the Gentiles, the Temple Mount was defiled, and
the people remained in exile.

The Muslims replaced the Christians as the religion in control of the
holy sites in Jerusalem. Apart from a short interval in the twelfth century, Muslim control of Jerusalem would remain until the twentieth
century. Islamic control of the Temple Mount continues to this day.

THERE WAS A NEW ATTITUDE TOWARD THE TEMPLE MOUNT

The conquering Muslims brought a different attitude with them. In
contrast to the Roman and Byzantine conquerors, which let the Temple
Mount remain in ruins as a proof of the destruction of Jewish national-
ism, the Muslims restored worship to the Mount. Yet the worship was
not of the Lord, the God of Israel, but of Allah, the God of Islam.

When the Muslims became the rulers in Jerusalem things became easier for the Jews. They were officially allowed to live in the city, and there is evidence that on certain holy days, they were permitted on the Temple Mount.

TEMPLE MOUNT ACTIVITY

Ancient reports say that the Jews would march in procession around the walls of the Temple Mount on feast days and pray at the gates. A document written in the tenth century indicates that one of the conditions for allowing the Jews to pray at the gates was that the Jewish community would be responsible for keeping the Temple Mount clean. The Jews, it states, were responsible to sweep the Mount. Other accounts indicate that Jews were employed in the mosque area and that Jewish craftsmen made lamps for the mosque.

Inscriptions have been found at the gates of the Temple Mount that were probably put there by Jewish Pilgrims during the early Arab rule. One such inscription, when translated, reads.

> You Lord of Hosts build this House in the lifetime of Jacob ben-Joseph, Theophylactus, and Sisinia and Anistasia. Amen and amen.

Though the Jews were allowed more access than in the Roman or Byzantine period, they were still far from their desired goal—retaking Jerusalem and the Temple Mount.

THE CRUSADERS CAPTURE JERUSALEM

In the last thirteen hundred years, with only one exception, the Temple Mount has been in the hands of Muslims. On July 15, 1099, the Crusaders from Europe took Jerusalem and the Temple Mount from the Muslims. The Crusaders slaughtered the inhabitants of Jerusalem in an unjustified carnage. The Dome of the Rock was converted into a Christian Church called the *Templum Domini*—Temple of our Lord.

Benjamin of Tudela, the famous Jewish traveler who visited Jerusalem in the twelfth century, wrote.

> Jerusalem has four gates: Abraham's Gate, David's Gate, the Zion Gate and the Gospat Gate, which is Jehoshaphat's Gate, in front of the Temple of ancient times. The *Templum Domini* now stands on the Temple site. On that spot Omar ibn al-Khattab built a large and exceedingly beautiful cupola. The gentiles do not take any image or picture into it but go there only to pray.

THE KNIGHTS HEADQUARTERS

The Al Aqsa Mosque was used as headquarters of the Knights of the Templar—those who officiated the Temple Compound. A remnant of the Crusader occupation still exists on the Temple Mount—the tombs of the assassins of Thomas Beckett, the Archbishop of Canterbury (1118-1170). After murdering Beckett, the assassins traveled to Jerusalem, and took up with the Templar Knights. Their tombs are situated near the main entrance to the Mosque.

The Western world rejoiced that Jerusalem, and its holy sites, were in the hands of "Christians." The victory, however, caused the Muslims to immediately launch campaigns to regain the city, and the Temple Mount, from the Christian infidels.

THE LEADER SALADIN

The Crusader occupation was relatively short-lived. The Muslim leader Saladin (Salah ad-Din) proclaimed a *jihad*, or holy war to retake the holy land. After ninety years of Crusader control, Jerusalem surrendered to Saladin's army on October 2, 1187. In contrast to the brutality of the Crusaders, Saladin treated the defeated Crusaders with kindness and mercy.

The golden cross that had been placed on the Dome of the Rock was torn down. Saladin rededicated the Templar's headquarters as a mosque. The Dome was covered with beautiful mosaics, and a prayer niche facing Mecca was added.

THE THIRD CRUSADE

With Jerusalem back in the hands of the Muslims Europe was ready to avenge the defeat. A Third Crusade was undertaken (1189-1192) to free Jerusalem from the armies of Saladin. But it would not succeed. Richard the Lion-hearted led England and other Crusaders in a fruitless attempt to retake the city. To this day, the Temple Mount remains in Muslim control.

THE CITY OF JERUSALEM BECOMES DESOLATE

The city of Jerusalem became a desolate place. In 1267, the Jewish sage Nahmanides wrote a letter to his son. It contained the following references to the land and the Temple.

> What shall I say of this land . . . The more holy the place the greater the desolation. Jerusalem is the most desolate of all . . . There are about 2,000 inhabitants . . . but there are no Jews, for after the arrival of the Tartars, the Jews fled, and some were killed by the sword. There are now only two brothers, dyers, who buy their dyes from the government. At their place a quorum of worshippers meets on the Sabbath . . . [they] found a ruined house, built on pillars, with a beautiful dome, and made it into a synagogue . . . People regularly come to Jerusalem, men and women from Damascus and from Aleppo and from all parts of the country, to see the Temple and weep over it. And may He who deemed us worthy to see Jerusalem in her ruins, grant us to see her rebuilt and restored, and the honor of the Divine Presence returned.

This desolation would continue for many centuries.

TURKISH RULE

The Ottoman Turks, non-Arab Muslims, became the dominant power in the 15th century. In 1453, they captured the city of Constantinople, and brought about the final destruction of the Eastern Roman Empire (Byzantine). They renamed the city Istanbul, and made it the center of their empire.

In 1517, under Sultan Selim I, the Turks captured Jerusalem and all of Israel. The rule of the Turks over Jerusalem would last exactly 400 years. The walls which today surround the Old City were built by Suleiman the Magnificent, son of Sultan Selim. Suleiman also restored the Al Aqsa Mosque. In fact, some of the present stained glass windows date from this period.

The Arabs found themselves under the domination of the Turks. For 400 years of Turkish rule, the Arabs did not have one independent state.

A REBUILDING REQUEST

There was a request for rebuilding the Temple during the Turkish period. The request read as follows.

> Since we have merited to these days, when such a great man as His Excellency has been appointed to Jacob, to whom every king stands at attention, perhaps the will of God will have success through him. And especially at a time like this, when the Land of Israel is under the dominion of the Pasha . . . perhaps if his most noble Excellency pays him a handsome sum and purchases for him some other country in exchange for the Holy Land, which is presently small in quantity but great in quality . . . this money would certainly not be wasted . . . for when the leaders of Israel are gathered from every corner of the world . . . and transform it into an inhabited country, then many God-fearing and charitable Jews will travel

there to take up their residence in the Holy Land under Jewish sovereignty . . . and be worthy to take their portion in the offering upon the altar. And if the master does not desire to sell the entire land, then at least he should sell Jerusalem and its environs . . . or at least the Temple Mount and surrounding areas . . . so that we may offer to the Lord our God.

Again, the request for the rebuilding of the Temple was denied.

NAPOLEON VISITS THE TEMPLE MOUNT

There is an account of Napoleon visiting the Temple Mount on the 9th of Av, the day of the commemoration of the Temple's destruction. When asked what all the crying and wailing was about, he was told that the Jews were mourning their Temple that had been destroyed 1800 years previously. Napoleon was moved with emotion at the things he saw. He said.

> A people which weeps and mourns for the loss of its homeland 1800 years ago and does not forget—such a people will never be destroyed. Such a people can rest assured that its homeland will be returned to it. The hope of the captives in Exile is that one day they would again come to their land, rebuild the Holy City, and their Temple.

NON-MUSLIMS ARE BARRED FROM THE MOUNT

J.T. Barclay, in the mid-19th century, wrote about the barring of those from the Mount who were not of the Islamic faith.

> When the clock of the Mosk needs repairing, they are compelled, however reluctantly, to employ a Frank. But in order to have a clean conscience in the commission of such an abominable piece of sacrilege as the admission upon the sacred premises, they adopt the following expedient. The mechanic selected being thoroughly purged from his

uncleanness ablution . . . a certain formula of prayer and incantation is sung over him at the gate. This being satisfactorily concluded, he is considered as exorcized, not only of Christianity (or Judaism, as the case may be), but of humanity also; and is declared to be no longer a man but a donkey. He is then mounted upon the shoulders of the faithful, lest . . . the ground should be polluted by his footsteps; and being carried to the spot where his labours are required, he is set down upon matting within certain prescribed limits; and the operation being performed, he is carried back to the gate, and there, by certain other ceremonies, he is duly *undonkeyfied* and transmuted back into a man again.[1]

THE PALESTINIAN EXPLORATION SOCIETY

From 1867 to 1870, under the auspices of the Palestinian Exploration Society, British engineer Charles Warren conducted a series of excavations around the outer wall of the Temple area. It was the first scientific study ever performed on the Temple area. Warren's work was heroic considering the dreadful conditions in which he had to work. No further scientific work would be done on the Temple Mount for another one hundred years.

THE DESOLATE LAND

The land continued to remain desolate. Mark Twain visited the Holy Land in 1867 and wrote the following description.

> [The Holy Land is] . . . a desolate country whose soil is rich enough, but is given over wholly to weeds—a silent mournful expanse . . . A desolation is here that not even imagination can grace with the pomp of life and action . . . We never saw a human being on the whole route . . . There was

---

1. Cited by Solomon Steckoll, *The Temple Mount*, London, Tom Stacey, Ltd., 1972, p. 31

hardly a tree or shrub anywhere. Even the olive and the cactus, those fast friends of a worthless soil, had almost deserted the country.[2]

THE TEMPLE MOUNT GAINS WORLDWIDE ATTENTION: THE SECRET DIG

At the beginning of the twentieth century, while the Turks were still ruling in Jerusalem, one of the biggest uproars that ever occurred around the Temple Mount happened—the ill-fated Parker expedition. Captain Montague Parker organized an expedition to Jerusalem to find a $200 million treasure that was supposedly hidden underneath the Temple. A Swedish philosopher, named Valter H. Juvelius, thought he found a coded passage in the book of Ezekiel that gave the location of this lost treasure. Since digging was not allowed on the Temple Mount, Parker and his group had to content themselves with digging around the area.

NO SECRET PASSAGE IS FOUND

After months of digging around the Temple Mount, no "secret passage" could be found. With their permit to dig about to expire, Parker bribed the Turkish governor to let him, and his cohorts, secretly dig on the Temple Mount. Dressed in Arab garb, the group came to the Mount at night and stealthily dug while it was dark. For about a week they continued this practice. However, just when they began to excavate the place where they believed the treasure to be, fate intervened. An attendant of the Mosque decided to sleep that night on the Temple Mount. Hearing strange noises coming from the Mosque he decided to investigate. He came upon Parker and his illegal dig. Immediately the horrified Muslim took to the streets to reveal this sacrilege. The result was a riot. The story continues.

> On the morning of April 19, 1911, a crowd of angry Muslims, outraged at what they considered to be a desecration of the

---

2. Mark Twain, *Innocents Abroad*, 1867

holy Mosque of Omar or the Dome of the Rock, rampaged through the streets of Jerusalem, quickly mobbing the entrance to the government citadel. The Turkish governor of the city, fearing for his own life at the hands of the crowd, ordered troops to quell the disturbance. But the soldiers were unable to control the growing mobs, and by nightfall, rioting and mayhem had spread to all parts of the city.

Never before had an archaeological expedition ended in so violent an uproar. But never before had there been an archaeological expedition quite like Captain Parker's. Conceived in folly, but planned with cunning, the Parker Mission had come to Jerusalem with a single goal: to locate and unearth the fantastic treasure of Solomon's Temple buried beneath the Temple Mount.[3]

Parker and his companions escaped with their live. This is another of the strange events that have occurred around the Temple and the Temple Mount.

THE JEW WITHOUT THE TEMPLE

During this time of their forced exile, the Jews continued to live without their Temple and sacrificial system. Jewish Christian author, Louis Goldberg, explains how the Jews compensated for the loss of the Temple.

> In the Hebrew Scriptures salvation is related to atonement, a sin offering, a Day of Atonement. While the combination of Scripture and tradition began to develop during the second Temple period, the presence of the Temple and priesthood still made possible a biblical demonstration of salvation. But after the second Temple was destroyed in 70 C.E., and

---

3. Neil Asher Silberman, In Search of Solomon's Lost Treasure, *Biblical Archaeological Review.* July/August, 1980, pp. 31-33

after the subsequent Dispersion of the Jewish people, Jewish scholars substituted for the Temple ritual of the sin offering and the Day of Atonement offerings the "three great concepts," which became in Orthodox and Conservative views the basis of righteousness. These concepts are repentance . . . prayer . . . and good deeds. These became the means by which one is made right with God and with his fellow man.[4]

Goldberg also notes.

After the Temple was destroyed, the substitution of these great concepts was introduced as dogma. Even before the Temple was gone, these were already a part of the life of the people; but after the place of sacrifice was destroyed, the three were regarded as equal to sacrifice.[5]

This was, and is, the state of things for the Jews without the Temple.

However, things were about to change for the Jews, the city of Jerusalem, and the possibility of building a new Temple.

SUMMARY TO CHAPTER 12

From the time of the destruction of the Second Temple in A.D. 70, the Jews have been wandering around the globe without a homeland. The holy city of Jerusalem and the Temple Mount remained in the control of others. As the twentieth century began, they were still a nation of people without a place to call home.

All of that was about to change. The monumental events of the twentieth century have begun the clock ticking toward the end of this age, and the Second Coming of Jesus Christ!

---

4. Louis Goldberg, *Our Jewish Friends*, Chicago, Moody Press, 1977, p. 88
5. Goldberg p. 88

PART 2

The Current State Of Jerusalem And The Temple Mount

We have considered the history of Jerusalem, the Jews, and the Temple Mount from their earliest history, to the twentieth century. Our next section will look at the present-day situation. We have already discovered the reasons why this Mount is so important to the three major religions. We are now going to look at the modern battle for the Temple Mount, and the right to worship on that sacred site.

CHAPTER 13

The Predicted Restoration of the Jews:
The Testimony of Scripture and History

But perhaps you say: "I don't believe the Israelites are to be restored to Canaan, and Jerusalem rebuilt." Dear reader have you read the declarations of God's word about it? Surely nothing is more plainly stated in Scripture.

William Blackstone, 1880[1]

Since the destruction of the Second Temple, the Jews had been exiled from their land, and scattered throughout the entire earth. No other nation in history (except the Jews themselves) has ever been totally removed from their homeland, and then restored. Yet the Bible says that God is not through with the nation Israel. Indeed, they have a future in His plans!

The predicted scattering and regathering of the Jews is not only a main topic of Scripture, those who have interpreted God's promises literally have also predicted it! The fact that Israel has not been permanently set aside in the plan of God, is clear from both the Old and New Testament. We will only cite a small portion of the relevant passages.

---

1. W.E. Blackstone, *Jesus is Coming*, Old Tappan New Jersey, Fleming Revell, reprint, 1932, p. 162

THE LAND IS AN EVERLASTING POSSESSION FOR ABRAHAM'S DESCENDANTS

God's promise to Abraham is that the land would belong to his descendants as an everlasting possession. The Lord said the following to him.

> All the land that you see I will give to you and your offspring forever (Genesis 13:15 NIV).

Later God repeated the promise.

> I will establish my covenant as an everlasting covenant between me and you and your descendants after you for the generations to come, to be your God and the God of your descendants after you. The whole land of Canaan, where you now reside as a foreigner, I will give as an everlasting possession to you and your descendants after you; and I will be their God (Genesis 17:7-8 NIV).

From these passages, as well as others, it is clear that ownership of the land belongs forever to Abraham's descendants. Their right to occupy the land is another matter.

JUDGMENT IS PROMISED FOR DISOBEDIENCE

The Bible had predicted the Lord would scatter His people, if they became disobedient to Him. We read in Deuteronomy.

> Then the LORD will scatter you among all nations, from one end of the earth to the other. There you will worship other gods—gods of wood and stone, which neither you nor your ancestors have known. Among those nations you will find no repose, no resting place for the sole of your foot. There the LORD will give you an anxious mind, eyes weary with longing, and a despairing heart. You will live in constant suspense, filled with dread both night and day, never sure of your life (Deuteronomy 28:64-66 NIV).

Judgment was promised to the people for their disobedience.

GOD WILL BRING THEM BACK TO THE LAND

Scripture also had predicted the Lord would bring them back. Again, we read about this in the Book of Deuteronomy. It says.

> When all these blessings and curses I have set before you come on you and you take them to heart wherever the LORD your God disperses you among the nations, and when you and your children return to the LORD your God and obey him with all your heart and with all your soul according to everything I command you today, then the LORD your God will restore your fortunes and have compassion on you and gather you again from all the nations where he scattered you (Deuteronomy 30:1-3 NIV).

IT WILL BE FOR HIS HOLY NAME

The return of the Jews to their land will be to honor God's holy name. The Lord spoke the following to the prophet Ezekiel.

> Son of man, when the people of Israel were living in their own land, they defiled it by their conduct and their actions. Their conduct was like a woman's monthly uncleanness in my sight. So I poured out my wrath on them because they had shed blood in the land and because they had defiled it with their idols. I dispersed them among the nations, and they were scattered through the countries; I judged them according to their conduct and their actions. And wherever they went among the nations they profaned my holy name, for it was said of them, 'These are the LORD's people, and yet they had to leave his land.' I had concern for my holy name, which the house of Israel profaned among the nations where they had gone. Therefore say to the house of Israel, 'This is what the Sovereign LORD says: It is not for your sake, house of Israel, that I am going to do these things, but for the sake of my holy name, which you have profaned among the

nations where you have gone. I will show the holiness of my great name, which has been profaned among the nations, the name you have profaned among them. Then the nations will know that I am the LORD, declares the Sovereign LORD, when I am proved holy through you before their eyes. 'For I will take you out of the nations; I will gather you from all the countries and bring you back into your own land' (Ezekiel 36:17-24 NIV).

This is very important to understand. God said that He will bring the people back to the land in order to honor *His* name. The nations will know that the Lord is God.

CONCLUSION: ABRAHAM'S DESCENDANTS OWN THE LAND

The Word of God is clear—the ownership of the land belongs to Abraham's descendants—their occupancy is based upon obedience. Because of disobedience, they have been exiled from their land. There will, however, be a final gathering of the Jews into their own land before Jesus Christ returns.

THE PREDICTIONS OF COMMENTATORS

There is also a long history of Bible commentators who, based upon the predictions of God's Word, have said the Jews must return someday to their land. This return will be in unbelief of Jesus as their Messiah. The regathering will occur before God's final judgment upon the earth, and the Second Coming of Jesus Christ. We will consider a few of the predictions of these past commentators.

In the seventeenth century, Bible scholar Increase Mather observed the following about the destiny of Israel.

> Some have believed and asserted a general conversion of the Jews, yet have doubted whether they should ever again possess the land of their fathers. But the Scripture is very clear

and full in this, that you see not how it can justly be denied or questioned. . . .A little before the conversion of the Jews, there will be the most terrible doings in the world that ever were heard of in respect of wars and commotions, the waves of the sea roaring, confused noise, and garments rolled in blood, blood and fire, and vapor of smoke; but after the kingdom shall be restored to Israel, then shall be glorious days of peace and tranquility.[2]

He noted that the Jews will be return to their land in the last days, experience the great tribulation, and then be converted.

John Gill wrote in the beginning of the eighteenth century. Concerning the Jews and the "last days" he penned the following words.

The land of Canaan, given to Abraham, etc. shall be again possessed by the Jews their posterity; for without supposing that the Jews upon their call and conversion to their own land, in a literal sense, I see not how we can understand this, and many other prophecies.[3]

Gill believed there would be a literal re-gathering of the Jews before the Lord returned.

Nineteenth century writer Thomas Scott put it this way.

As this is here introduced subsequent to the calling of the Gentiles, it evidently foretells the future calling of the tribes of Israel . . . and their restoration to their own land. That in the latter days they shall actually return from their several dispersions, to dwell as a nation in their own land, is declared

2. Increase Mather, *The Mystery of Israel's Salvation—concerning the Conversion of the Israelitish Nation*, London, 1669, pp. 12, 53,57
3. John Gill: *"An Exposition of the Old and New Testament,"* London, 1810, Vol. I, p. 133

in such express terms by most of the ancient prophets, that there cannot be a doubt, I think, of its being literally accomplished in due time.[4]

He also looked for a literal fulfillment in the last days of the nation of Israel returning to its own land.

Bible teacher James H. Brookes compares the prediction of the destruction of Jerusalem with a literal future restoration of the people.

> The disciples could not possibly have understood our Lord to mean anything but the literal Jerusalem where they stood when He uttered the prediction [of its destruction] . . . They were compelled to understand Him as speaking of the literal Jerusalem. But if so, it is certain they would anticipate a restoration of the city of the Israelites, for our Lord says, "Jerusalem shall be trodden down of the Gentiles until the times of the Gentiles be fulfilled." There is no meaning in the language unless the word until implies that a time is coming, when Jerusalem shall cease to be trodden down of the Gentiles; but after the lapse of more than eighteen hundred years, we know that the time is not yet, because the times of the Gentiles are not yet run out. Various attempts have been made to set aside this prediction, all of which, of course, have resulted in ignominious failure; for it is not the rash utterance of a crazed enthusiast, nor the crafty speech of a base impostor, but the sad and solemn announcement of God manifest in the flesh.[5]

This writer makes a number of excellent points. If language means anything, then we should look for a literal fulfillment of the Jews

---

4. Thomas Scott, *The Holy Bible Containing the Old and New Testaments*, Volume IV, Boston, Samuel T. Armstrong, Third Boston and Ninth American Edition, 1823, p. 238

5. James H. Brookes, *Maranatha or The Lord Cometh*, St. Louis, Edward Brendell Publisher, 1931, p. 218

returning to their own land shortly before the coming of the Lord. Indeed, this is how Jesus' immediate disciples would have understood these words. Furthermore, it is God the Son, not some crazed person, who made these predictions.

In sum, before the Second Coming of Christ, we should look for the national return of the Jews to their ancient homeland.

In the nineteenth century, W.E. Blackstone made the following comment about the future of Israel.

> If Israel is beginning to show signs of national life and is actually returning to Palestine, then sure the end of this dispensation is nigh, even at the doors.[6]

Israel is the key. Indeed, when the nation shows signs of life then we should expect the coming of the Lord to occur soon afterward.

J. H. Kurtz made this insightful observation about the relationship of the nation of Israel to its land.

> As the body is adapted and designed for the soul, and the soul for the body; so is Israel for that country and that country for Israel. Without Israel, the land is like a body from which the soul has fled; banished from its country, Israel is like a ghost which cannot find rest.[7]

The people of Israel cannot find rest until they return home.

A Bible teacher from the nineteenth century, John Cumming, wrote about the necessity of the return of the Jews to their ancient homeland. He put it this way.

---

6. W.E. Blackstone, *Jesus is Coming*, Old Tappan New Jersey, Fleming Revell reprint, 1932, p. 81

7. J.H. Kurtz, *"History of the Old Covenant,"* English Translation, Philadelphia, 1859, Vol. I, p. 44

The Jews were the only nation upon earth for whom God selected and consecrated a land. For them he chose the land of Canaan, and to them we read he gave it for a possession forever. He selected no land for the Greek, no territory for the Roman; but for his people Israel he selected a land and to that people in the fullness of time he made it over. To them he has still promised it, in words that are not exhausted as a possession and a heritage forever.[8]

Again we find the emphasis on the Promised Land and the necessity of the nation to someday return to their ancient homeland.

The Importance Of Jerusalem

Ancient writers also understood the importance of the city of Jerusalem in the "last days" scenario. Nineteenth century author E.W. Bullinger wrote.

The manifestation of the Lord in Glory—the national forgiveness of Israel—the destruction of the great and glorious power of the Gentiles that will, till then have flourished—the introduction of the new age of blessing—are all connected with an event yet to happen in the history of Jerusalem. A future event in Jerusalem's history becomes the great turning point of the destinies of the earth. The great coming crisis in the earth's history is seen to be connected, not with Rome and the papacy, nor with Constantinople and Mahomet, but with Jerusalem . . . The more I examined Scripture, the more I was convinced that it teemed with evidence that not merely of Jerusalem being the place where the last great confederacy of evil will meet its doom, but that it was also

---

8. John Cumming, *The Great Consummation*, New York, Carlton Publishers, 1864, p. 112

the place around which the preceding events, that give to the close to this dispensation its character revolve as their centre.[9]

In other words, Jerusalem will be center-stage for the events in the last day.

THE JEWS WILL COME BACK IN UNBELIEF

There is something else that we should be aware of. The Scripture says the Jews must return to their ancient homeland in "unbelief" of Jesus.

In the 19th century, learned commentator B.W. Newton was led to conclude that the Bible called for a re-gathering of the Jews to their land in unbelief. Newton recognized that this future re-gathering of the Jews was a clear part of God's plan. He wrote.

> Circumstances however, occurred that led me to consider with care the eleventh chapter of Romans. I could not close my eyes to the fact that the future history of Israel of the literal Israel was there spoken of. . . . I saw that it could be explained only of the future forgiveness of Israel as a nation. I saw also that Israel when nationally converted, are not to be merged in the present Gentile Church.[10]

Elsewhere he wrote.

> First, from these chapters [Zechariah 12-14] we learn that the Jews as a nation will be converted and forgiven, *when they are in their own land and city* (italics his). Therefore it follows that they must return to their land and city *when uncoverted.*[11]

---

9. E. W. Bullinger, *The Apocalypse or "The Day of the Lord"*, Third Edition, Revised and Corrected, London, Eyre and Spottiswoode, 1935, p. 94

10. B.W. Newton, How B.W. *Newton Learned Prophetic Truth*, London, Sovereign Grace Advent Testimony, 1880, p. 4

11. B.W. Newton, p. 10

Newton stressed that the Bible predicted the Jews would return to their ancient homeland in an unconverted state.

THEY WILL RETURN BEFORE THE GREAT TRIBULATION

Eighteenth century commentator Elhanan Winchester emphasized the same truth. He put it this way.

> We may be sure that the Jews will not be converted before their return to their own land. And it has been a very great, though general mistake, to suppose that their conversion would first take place, in order for their return; whereas this terrible calamity that shall fall upon them, supposes the contrary. For is it reasonable to suppose, that God would thus deliver up his beloved people, when they had newly returned to him, into the hands of their cruel foes, who should thus be permitted to exercise such horrible brutality upon them?.[12]

Winchester's point is well taken. According to Jesus, the great tribulation will occur before He returns. Christ said this would be the worst time of judgment the world would ever experience. Consequently, God would not subject His people to this time of punishment, if they had been newly converted. On the contrary, the time of their conversion will be a time of blessing. Therefore, they will return in unbelief *before* their national conversion.

MANY MORE REFERENCES COULD BE ADDED

This is a small sampling of the testimony of commentators concerning the future of the Jews as predicted in Scripture. Let us remember they were making these predictions—that the Jews will return to their land in unbelief of Jesus—while the nation was still in exile, and had been in exile for eighteen centuries!

---

12. Elhanan Winchester, *A Course of Lectures on the Prophecies Which Remain to Be Fulfilled*, (delivered in 1788-1790) Cincinnati: E. Morgan and Company, 1851, p. 125

Yet, against all odds of history, these commentators, based upon a literal understanding of the Bible, predicted the Jews would someday return to their land.

IT HAS NEVER HAPPENED BEFORE

This type of return, a people coming back to their homeland once they had been removed, had never happened once in the history of the world—except for the Jews themselves returning from the Babylonian captivity (606-536 B.C.). Yet these commentators believed the return must someday happen—because the Bible says so!

SUMMARY TO CHAPTER 13

The testimony of Scripture is clear. The Jews must return to their land in unbelief of Jesus as their Messiah before God's program is complete.

Careful Bible students have noted this for the last two thousand years, and have predicted this restoration.

Though it seemed impossible to come to pass, as we shall see, the impossible has indeed happened!

CHAPTER 14

1948: God's Word is Fulfilled Again: The Modern State of Israel is Reborn!

By the rivers of Babylon we sat and wept when we remembered Zion. There on the poplars we hung our harps, for there our captors asked us for songs, our tormentors demanded songs of joy; they said, "Sing us one of the songs of Zion!" How can we sing the songs of the LORD while in a foreign land? If I forget you, Jerusalem, may my right hand forget its skill. May my tongue cling to the roof of my mouth if I do not remember you, if I do not consider Jerusalem my highest joy.

(Psalm 137:1-6)

We have seen the fulfillment of God's promises in allowing the Jews to return to their land after seventy years of captivity in Babylon. As God had promised, those who returned from exile rebuilt the city of Jerusalem, and the Temple. The long-awaited Messiah came to the Second Temple, and was rejected. Jesus pronounced judgment on the city, the Temple, and the people. All His words were literally fulfilled.

The Scriptures also spoke of their return to the Promised Land, and to Jerusalem. The twentieth century has witnessed the fulfillment of these ancient prophecies of the return of the Jews to Israel—testifying to the truth of the Word of God. We will briefly recount their amazing story.

THEODORE HERZL AND MODERN ZIONISM

In January, 1895, a Jewish Austrian journalist named Theodor Herzl, covered the trial in Paris of a French Jew named Dreyfus. Dreyfus was unfairly convicted of a crime that he did not commit. Seeing the hatred directed against Jews, Herzl determined to begin a process to found a Jewish state. Later in 1895, Herzl published a book entitled *Der Judenstaat—The Jewish State*. He argued that the only way in which the "Jewish problem" can be resolved was by establishing a Jewish state in the Holy Land. Herzl's writings started the Jews on the road back to their Promised homeland.

At the conclusion of the First Zionist Congress in Basel, Switzerland (September 3, 1897), Theodore Herzl made the following entry into his diary.

> In Basel I founded the Jewish State. If I said this aloud, it would be greeted with worldwide derision. In five years, perhaps, and certainly in fifty, everyone will see it.

Herzl's entry in his diary would turn out to be prophetic.

A PROPOSED HOMELAND IN UGANDA

In 1903, the British proposed to the Jews that they settle in the African country of Uganda. This was rejected by representatives of the people. England's offer was, however, recognition that the Jews had a right to a homeland. To the Jews there is only one place on earth that they would make as their homeland—the land that God had promised to Abraham as their everlasting possession.

TURKISH RULE ENDS IN THE HOLY LAND

The four-hundred-year reign over the Holy Land, by the Ottoman Turks, was about to end. During World War I, the Arabs helped the British fight the Turks. D.E. Lawrence, "Lawrence of Arabia," was instrumental in achieving the victory over the Ottoman Empire.

In October 1917, a British General, Edmund Allenby, launched an invasion in the Holy Land. On Sunday, December 9th, the Turks were driven out of Jerusalem. Two days later, the General made his entry into conquered Jerusalem, on foot. He said no one could enter the Holy City except in humility on foot. He said upon entering.

> Since your city is regarded with affection by the adherents of three great religions of mankind, and its soil has been consecrated by the prayers and the pilgrimages of devout people of these three religions for many centuries, therefore I do make known to you . . . that all sacred buildings will be maintained and protected according to the existing customs and beliefs of those whose faiths are sacred.

At the conclusion of the First World War, Britain, France, and Russia forged the Sykes-Picot Agreement. This pact carved up the Ottoman Empire which had seen its defeat in the War. Britain gained control of the Holy Land. For the first time in 800 years, the Holy sites of Christianity were delivered from the domination of Islam.

THE REQUEST OF CHAIM WEITZMAN

Another step toward the realization of a Jewish homeland came after the First World War. Chaim Weitzman, a brilliant Jewish chemist, helped the War effort by developing a technique where synthetic acetone could be manufactured. Acetone was a prime ingredient in the production of explosives. His discovery was given credit by the British government as a main factor in Britain winning the War. The government attempted to personally reward him for his efforts on behalf of the nation. Weitzman asked nothing for himself, but he did make a request for his people—a Jewish homeland in Palestine.

A JEWISH HOMELAND IS PROPOSED

Weitzman's request for a Jewish homeland probably led to the most significant step toward that goal—the Balfour Declaration. On November

2, 1917, British Foreign Secretary Lord Balfour, wrote a letter to a representative of the Jewish people—Baron Edward de Rothchild. The British government, in this Balfour declaration, pledged its support for the establishment of a homeland for the Jews in Palestine.

> His majesty's Government view with favour the establishment in Palestine of a national home for the Jewish people, and will use their best endeavors to facilitate the achievement of this objective, it being clearly understood that nothing shall be done which may prejudice the civil and religious rights of existing and non-Jewish communities in Palestine, or the rights and political status enjoyed by Jews in any other country.

The Balfour Declaration set the stage for the modern state of Israel to be born. This declaration did not please the Arabs. Since they had helped the British oust the Turks, they expected to receive full control of the Holy Land. They saw the Balfour declaration as a betrayal. Britain responded by saying that Arab independence did not include the Holy Land.

A PLANNED ATTACK AGAINST THE DOME?

The Holy Land, now under British rule, began to experience further bloodshed. In 1929, agents of the Grand Mufti began spreading false rumors among the Palestinian Arabs that the Jews planned to attack their holy shrine—the Dome of the Rock. An armed Arab mob, inflamed by these claims, descended upon the Jewish part of Jerusalem on August 23, 1929. During the following week, the violence spread throughout the entire country. By the time British reinforcements arrived, 133 Jews had been killed, as well as 116 Arabs. Jerusalem's Temple Mount was again at the center of the controversy.

WORLD WAR II—THE NAZI HOLOCAUST

During the Second World War, the Jews experienced their worst tragedy to date. Six million Jews were put to death under the regime of

Adolph Hitler. Hitler, like other anti-Semites, attempted to use the death of Jesus as his reason for persecuting the Jews. In a speech he gave on April 12, 1922, Hitler said.

> In boundless love, as a Christian and a human being, I read the passage which tells us how the Lord at last rose in His might and seized the scourge to drive out of the Temple the brood of vipers and adders. How terrific was His fight against the Jewish poison; I realize more profoundly than ever before the fact that it was for this that He had to shed his blood upon the Cross.[1]

During the Second World War it looked as though there was going to be the complete annihilation of the Jewish race. Yet Hitler's attempt to destroy the Jews, like other tyrants in the past, miserably failed. The Jews survived the Holocaust with an increasing desire to have their own homeland.

THE UNITED NATIONS PARTITION IN 1947

The Jews' struggle for their own homeland was eventually victorious. The British finally gave up trying to administrate the Holy Land. They turned the problem over to the United Nations on April 2, 1947.

On November 29, 1947, the United Nations voted the right of the Jewish people to have their own homeland. The United Nations voted to partition the land into two states: one for the Palestinian Arabs, and the other for the Jews.

This vote was exactly fifty years after the Zionist Conference of 1897. Herzl's diary entry was correct—50 years from his time the whole world would indeed see the Jewish state.

---

1. "Hitler on Jesus," *Christian Jewish Relations*, Volume 16, No. 4, 1983, p. 60

THE MODERN STATE OF ISRAEL IS BORN

On May 14, 1948, against all the odds, the modern state of Israel was reborn. At four o'clock that afternoon, the members of the provisional national council, led by David Ben-Gurion, met in the Tel Aviv Art Museum. Ben-Gurion rose and read the following proclamation to the assembled guests.

> The Land of Israel was the birthplace of the Jewish people. Here their spiritual, religious and national identity was formed. Here they achieved independence and created a culture of national and universal significance. Here they wrote and gave the Bible to the world.

> Exiled from Palestine, the Jewish people remained, faithful to it in all countries of their dispersion, never ceasing to pray and hope for their return and the restoration of their national freedom. . .

> Accordingly we, the members of the National Council, representing the Jewish people in Palestine and the Zionist movement of the world, met together in solemn assembly today, the day of the termination of the British Mandate of Palestine, by virtue of the natural and historic right of the Jewish people and the Resolution of the General Assembly of the United Nations, hereby proclaim the establishment of the Jewish state in Palestine, to be called ISRAEL . . .

With trust in Almighty God, we set our hand to this declaration, at this session of the Provisional State Council, in the city of Tel Aviv, on this Sabbath eve, the fifth of Iyar, 5708, the fourteenth day of May, 1948.

One writer put it this way.

> The shock of this terrible disaster [World War II] finally gave the Jews the power of desperation so that against the logic

of history and politics, a mere three years after the greatest catastrophe in their history, came one of their greatest triumphs: on May 15, 1948, the State of Israel was established.

THE WAR OF INDEPENDENCE FOLLOWED

The Arab leaders had promised they would invade the Holy Land and crush the Jews as soon as the British Mandate was over. The armies of Egypt, Syria, and Iraq were poised on the border—ready to deliver the death blow to the newly formed state. The Jordanian army already held strategic positions within the Holy Land.

From the Jewish perspective, the situation looked hopeless. This fledgling nation had no planes, tanks, or artillery to repel a full-scale invasion. In addition, there was no place for them to retreat. It looked as though this newly formed state would die in its infancy.

As promised, the new state of Israel was attacked by Arab forces as soon as their independence was declared. The result was an amazing victory for Israel, and a staggering defeat for their Arab enemies. Time magazine reported on this military victory.

> Out of the concentration camps, ghettos, courtrooms, theatres and factories of Europe the Chosen People had assembled and won their first great military victory since 166-160 B.C. Israel's victory came after the worst of a thousand persecutions.[2]

The Jews had not only returned to their ancient homeland, they survived a war that they seemed certain to lose.

THE TEMPLE MOUNT STILL IN ARAB HANDS

The prophecies had come to pass. The Jews were now back in their own land, but there was still more land to be obtained. The Jews did not

---

2. *Time*, August 16, 1948

control the Old City of Jerusalem that includes the Temple Mount, and the Western Wall.

In 1948, full Muslim control and Islamic rule was returned to these areas of Jerusalem when King Abdullah took them in the War of Independence.

For the next 19 years, the Temple Mount and the Western Wall would be in the hands of the Arabs. The only Jews that could visit these sites had to have good passports that were issued outside of Israel. Only a small amount of people came to visit.

THE AL-AQSA ASSASSINATION

The Temple Mount found itself in the headlines in the early years of the Jewish state. On Friday, June, 13, 1951, King Abdullah of Transjordan was assassinated at the entrance of the Al Aqsa Mosque. A bullet scarred pillar just inside the entrance of the Mosque still serves as a reminder of this tragic event.

One of the bullets deflected and almost killed his grandson, the former ruler of Jordan, the late King Hussein. King Hussein took over the rule at the age of seventeen. He was the first person to fully lift restrictions to non-Muslims to visit the enclosures and the interior of the Dome of the Rock, and the Al Aqsa Mosque.

THE CITY OF JERUSALEM IS DIVIDED

From 1948 to 1967, the city of Jerusalem remained divided. Tensions were constantly running high on both sides. It was only a matter of time until the people would experience another war—for total control of the Holy City and the Temple Mount.

SUMMARY TO CHAPTER 14

The twentieth century has seen the attempted annihilation of the Jews in the Nazi Holocaust. However, three years after World War II ended, the modern State of Israel was reborn. All this has been anticipated by Scripture. The cities lying in rubble were rebuilt as Jews came from all over the world to live again in their ancient homeland.

The Holy City of Jerusalem was not completely in their hands—being partitioned between the Israelis and the Arabs. The Temple Mount remained in the control of the Muslims. Between 1948 and 1967, the area of the Temple Mount was off limits to Israelis.

The liberation of the Old City, and the Temple Mount, would have to wait another 19 years.

CHAPTER 15

1967: Setting the Stage Further: Jerusalem Reunited Under Israeli Rule

Many different men other than the Jews have been in the seat of power—Jebusites, Egyptians, Babylonians and Persians; Hellenistic Greeks and Romans; Byzantines, Arabs, Crusaders, Mamelukes, Turks and British. But throughout the flux of these thousands of years there runs one constant thread—the unique attachment of the Jewish people to Jerusalem and the site of their holy Temple. History has no parallel to this mystic bond, and without it there would have been no state of Israel today.

Joan Comay[1]

In 1967, when attacked by the Jordanians, the Jews were willing to sacrifice their lives for Jerusalem. They would again. Some would give up . . . the Golan, the Sinai, the West Bank. But I do not think you will find any Israelis who are willing to give up Jerusalem. This beautiful golden city is the heart and soul of the Jewish people. You cannot live without a heart and soul. If you want one word to symbolize all of Jewish history, that word would be Jerusalem.

Israeli paratrooper, 1967[2]

1. Joan Comay, *The Temple At Jerusalem*, New York, Holt, Rhinehart, 1975, p. 163
2. Kibbutz Members, eds. *The Seventh Day*, London, 1974, p. 135

After the United Nations recognition of Israel in 1948, and the War of Independence that immediately followed, the city of Jerusalem remained divided between Jews and Arabs. All the eyes of the world were upon this city that has been sieged about forty different times, and has been destroyed, at least partially, on thirty-two different occasions.

The city of Jerusalem, the home promised to the descendants of Abraham, Isaac, and Jacob was about to return into the possession of the Jews.

THE TEMPLE MOUNT IS LIBERATED

In June 1967, another war broke out between Israel and their Arab neighbors—the Six Day War. This conflict resulted in the liberation of the holy places in the Old City of Jerusalem—including the Temple Mount.

On the third day of the Six Day War, Israeli Paratroop Commander, Motta Gur, mounted on a halftrack, announced that the Temple Mount had been regained. The ancient site of the Holy Temple was once again in Jewish hands!

JERUSALEM IS REUNIFIED

On June 7, 1967, the Israeli troops moved into the Old City and stood at the Western Wall (Wailing Wall) for prayer. Rabbi Shlomo Goren declared.

> We have taken the city of God. We are entering the Messianic era for the Jewish people, and I promise . . . that what we are responsible for we will take care of.

The city of Jerusalem was reunified and the Star of David flew again from its ramparts.

THIS EVENT FULFILLED BIBLE PROPHECY

The retaking of the entire city of Jerusalem by the Israelis is a further fulfillment of last days' prophecy.

Arnold Fruchtenbaum writes.

> The Jewish Temple will be rebuilt and will begin to func-
> tion again, for these verses view the Jewish Temple as having
> been rebuilt and functioning. These verses also presuppose
> Jewish control of the Temple Compound, and that presup-
> poses Jewish control over the Old City of Jerusalem. While
> none of these factors spell out a time factor as to when this
> will occur, it was clearly fulfilled in the Six Day War. While
> the Six Day War itself was never predicted in the Scriptures,
> what it accomplished certainly was. The Six Day War
> brought about the fulfillment of the prophecy regarding the
> Jewish control of the Old City of Jerusalem.[3]

It seemed that these events in 1967 set the stage for the rebuilding of
the Temple. However, it was not to be.

THE CONTROL OF THE TEMPLE MOUNT WAS GIVEN BACK TO THE MUSLIMS

The Temple Mount was back in the hands of the Israelis! In a sign of
victory, the Israeli army raised their flag on the Dome of the Rock.
On the same day, Israeli Defense Minister, Moshe Dayan, ordered it
removed.

Ten days after the conclusion of the Six Day War, an extraordinary
gesture of good will was made concerning the Temple Mount. This
gesture was provided by the Israelis to the Muslim religious leaders of
Jerusalem. On Saturday, June 17, 1967, Moshe Dayan entered the Al
Aqsa Mosque for a historic meeting with five leaders of the Supreme
Muslim Council—the men who had formerly controlled the Temple
Mount. Dayan sat down with these leaders on a prayer carpet and dis-
cussed the Temple Mount and its future administration. The meeting

3. Arnold Fruchtenbaum, *Israelology: The Missing Link in Systematic Theology*, Ariel
Ministries, Tustin, California, 1992, pp. 766-767

that day set Israel's policy regarding the Temple Mount—a policy that remains to this day.

The discussion with the Muslims led to Israeli concessions concerning the Temple Mount. The administrative control over the Temple Mount was to be the sole responsibility of the Supreme Muslim Council—the Waqf. Though the Jews would be permitted free access to the Mount, prayer, or public worship, by Jews was prohibited.

THERE IS NO JEWISH IDENTIFICATION ON THE TEMPLE MOUNT

Dayan refused to permit any Jewish identification with Judaism's holiest site. To him, the Temple Mount held only historic interest. He said.

> I have no doubt that because the power is in our hands we must take a stand based on yielding. We must view the Temple Mount as a historic site relating to past memory.

WHY WAS IT GIVEN BACK TO THE MUSLIMS?

Since the destruction of the Second Temple, some two thousand years ago, every Orthodox Jew prays three times a day for the Lord to rebuild the Temple. The symbolic breaking of a glass at a Jewish wedding also serves as a reminder that their Temple has been destroyed. Why then, did the Jews give back the administration of the Mount as soon as they took control over it?

THREE REASONS FOR GIVING MUSLIMS CONTROL OF THE MOUNT

Three basic reasons can be given for the Jews turning back the administration of the Temple Mount to the Muslims. They are as follows.

1) The Status Quo Policy

2) The Holy Of Holies Issue

3) Potential Muslim Reaction

1. THE STATUS QUO POLICY

The basis for the State of Israel leaving the authority of the Temple Mount with the Muslims goes back to an 18th century policy known as the "Status Quo." Simply stated, though the rule over a country may change hands, the Christian holy places would remain under the authority of those who had been overseeing it. In other words, the holy places would keep the "Status Quo."

At that time, there was conflict between the Roman Catholic and Orthodox churches over the Christian Holy Places. International political pressure was placed upon the Turkish rulers of the Holy Land to resolve the conflict. Thus, in 1757, the Turks issued a legal decree defining the rights of Christian groups in the various Holy Places. This set the policy of the Status Quo.

THE STATUS QUO IS UPHELD

In 1852, a decree was issued by the Turkish Sultan Abduk Mejid. This provided the most complete description of the policy of the Status Quo. At the Treaty of Paris in 1855, the policy of the Status Quo was upheld by the major European nations. At the end of the Russian-Turkish war in 1878, the Treaty of Vienna was signed. The Treaty stated that no change shall be made in the Status Quo without the permission of the signatories.

When the Holy Sites came under the control of Britain in 1917, the conquering General Allenby announced that they would continue the policy of the Status Quo at the Holy Places.

After the War of Independence in 1948, the control of the Holy Places was in the hands of Transjordan. From 1948 to 1967, they continued to enforce the policy of the Status Quo.

In 1967, the Israelis captured the Holy Places in Jerusalem. Although the Status Quo had reference to only Christian Holy Sites, the Israeli government decided to continue the policy rather than attempting to implement a change.

In the case of the Temple Mount, it meant that the Jews would relinquish any claims to its administration because the Muslims had been the previous caretakers of this Holy Site. This policy has kept the Jews from having any authority on the Temple Mount, and has made, for the present time, the idea of building a Third Temple a virtual impossibility.

2. THE HOLY OF HOLIES QUESTION

Another thing that has helped to minimize tensions between Jews and Arabs concerning the Temple Mount is a ban on its entrance by the Chief Rabbinate of Israel. The Orthodox Rabbinate prohibits Jews from entering the site because of the possibility that they might step on a Holy Place. Since the precise location of the Temple, and the Holy of Holies, is unknown, there is fear that a visitor may unsuspectingly step on the holy site. Though the ban does not carry any legal weight, it does keep some religious Jews from entering the Mount.

At the entrance to the Temple Mount the following sign is posted as a warning to Jews.

NOTICE AND WARNING

Entrance to the area of the Temple Mount is forbidden to everyone by Jewish Law owing to the sacredness of the place.

The Chief Rabbinate of Israel

The orthodox Jews generally observe the ban, while other Jews do not. The reason for the ban is that Gentiles, as well as Jews, are regarded as "unclean" today, and are thus unfit to walk on the sacred Mount. The Temple Mount is considered so sacred that one is forbidden even to fly over it—because the holiness of the site extends into the heavens. Therefore, the orthodox Jew is allowed only to admire the Temple

Mount from a distance. This ban will stay in effect until the Messiah comes. Because of the ban, the Jews worship at the Western Wall or "Wailing Wall" below the Temple Mount.

Since Orthodox Jews cannot enter the site, the requests by Jewish groups to hold organized prayer are considered political demonstrations, and not prayer services—the Temple Mount, as a Holy Place, is not an appropriate place for political demonstrations.

3. THE FEAR OF MUSLIM RIOTS

A third reason why the control of the Temple Mount remains with the Muslims is the realistic fear by the Israeli government of Muslims riots, or something worse. Every inch of land held by Islam is considered holy Islamic soil, and its possession by the infidels (Christians or Jews) is inadmissible, intolerable, a blasphemy, and a cause for *jihad* (holy war). No compromise or concession is ever possible.

This fact has kept the Israeli officials from tampering with the Muslim authority over the Temple Mount. Among the Israelis in power, there is a strong desire not to alienate the Muslim world. The goal is to preserve public order.

FREEDOM OF WORSHIP IS GUARANTEED

After the city of Jerusalem was reunified, the Knesset (Israeli Parliament), passed a law which guaranteed freedom of access and worship in all the holy sites. This is enforced with one notable exception—the Temple Mount. Though freedom of worship is guaranteed, any open display of worship is not allowed. The carrying of a prayer book, or the attempt to pray on the Mount, is not allowed. The police believe that such an act is a threat to the peace because of Muslim reaction. Hence the Temple Mount is treated differently than all the rest of the holy sites in Israel.

THERE IS NO FREEDOM OF WORSHIP ON THE MOUNT

The consequence of the Muslim Administration of the Temple Mount is that there is no freedom of worship for either Jews or Christians on that site. The Ministry of Religious Affairs has not been sympathetic to those who wish freedom of worship on the Temple Mount. On June 27, 1967, the day the law regarding the Holy Places was adopted, the Minister of Religious Affairs said, "It is our standing afar and our disinclination to enter, that illustrates our awe and reverence over the site of our former Temples."

PERMISSION IS DENIED TO PERMIT WORSHIP ON THE MOUNT

On a number of different occasions, the High Court of Justice has heard pleas from Jews to permit freedom of worship on the Temple Mount. Each time the requests have been denied. In addition, the current Supreme Muslim Council looks to a 1931 decision that the Temple Mount is exclusive Waqf property. The Waqf, who owes their allegiance to Jordan, does not accept the reunification of Jerusalem.

THE MOUNT IS KEPT OFF LIMITS

These three factors, the policy of the Status Quo, the unknown site of the Temple and the Holy of Holies, and the fear of Muslim retribution, has kept the Temple Mount in Muslim control, and off limits to Israelis.

Israeli citizens have been largely apathetic about the Temple Mount ruling. Within the various religious factions, there is no consensus of opinion about the holiness of the Temple Mount.

THE WESTERN WALL: THE WAILING WALL

Lacking the Temple Mount, the Jews congregate today at the Western Wall. The Western Wall is a quarter-mile long retaining wall that formed the western boundary of the Temple Mount. A 185 foot exposed section is an open air prayer area—also known as the "Wailing Wall." The

Western Wall was not part of the Temple. It was, rather, one of the four retaining walls that surrounded the Temple Mount, supporting the platform on which the Temple formerly stood.

THIS ADDITION WAS BUILT BY KING HEROD

Herod the Great built the Western Wall in order to enlarge the Temple Mount. Herod wanted to enlarge the worship area, beautify it, and add more buildings to the Temple complex. When the Romans destroyed the Temple in A.D. 70, they left standing this retaining wall to commemorate the magnitude of their victory. It is the only remaining portion of the Second Temple complex—but the Wailing Wall is not a substitution for the Temple. Rabbi Chaim Richman explains.

> When a Jew prays, "May the Temple be rebuilt speedily in our days," he is praying for the rebuilding of the Temple on the Temple Mount and, in Jewish tradition, that event when it happens, will herald a new world with the coming of the Messiah. These utopian and messianic hopes are focused on the Temple and not on the Western Wall or any other secondary structure in the area. Prayer at the Wall became important as a result of compromise—because the Temple is not rebuilt—but cannot, in any way serve to transfer the spotlight from the center to the periphery. No matter how holy its traditions have become, the Wall cannot be a substitute for the Temple and should not contribute to the demise of the Jewish people's messianic aspirations.[4]

THE TEMPLE MOUNT TODAY

On the Temple Mount stand the two famous structures, the Dome of the Rock and the Al Aqsa Mosque. They both stand high upon the Temple Mount, providing to the Jews a constant reminder that "pagan" holy places are on the site where their sacred Temple stood.

---

4. Chaim Richman, *The Odyssey Of The Third Temple*

The words of the Lord, through the prophet Ezekiel, are as true today as ever.

> I will bring the most wicked of nations to take possession of their houses. I will put an end to the pride of the mighty, and their sanctuaries will be desecrated. . . . This is what the Sovereign LORD says: The enemy said of you, "Aha! The ancient heights have become our possession" (Ezekiel 7:24; 36:2 NIV).

The holy place, the Temple Mount, is indeed in the hands of unbelievers.

MUSLIM CLAIMS TO THE MOUNT

To make matters worse, Islam claims that the Temple Mount complex is "their" holy place. Indeed, the official guidebook to the Al-Aqsa Mosque repeats the Muslim claim that the Temple Mount, or the Noble Sanctuary as they call it, is the third holiest site in their religion. Their official Al-Aqsa Mosque guidebook says.

> The Al-Aqsa Mosque building and the Dome of the Rock, and many religious and educational institutions and shrines which have been established within Al-Aqsa throughout its nearly 1400-year history, are all a testament to the love and respect that all Muslims have for this site, one of the three most sacred places on earth for Islam.

Therefore, not only is this sacred site not in the hands of the Israelis, it is operated by another religion which claims it is *their* sacred site.

A DENIAL OF JEWISH PRESENCE

In addition, we find that the official Al-Aqsa Mosque guidebook denies that there was ever any Jewish presence on the Temple Mount. It says the following.

> The beauty and tranquility of Al-Aqsa Mosque in Jerusalem attracts thousands of visitors of all faiths every year. Some

believe it was the site of the Temple of Solomon, peace be upon him, destroyed by Nebuchadnezzar in 587 BC, or the site of the Second Temple, completely destroyed by the Romans in 70 AD, although no documented historical or archaeological evidence exists to support this.

To the Muslims, there never has been a Jewish presence on the Temple Mount, only an Islamic presence.

THE MUSLIMS BELIEVE THE ENTIRE MOUNT IS A MOSQUE

Prior to 1967, the central structure on the Mount for the Muslims was the Al Aqsa Mosque. After the city was recaptured in 1967, the Waqf began to term the entire Temple Mount as Al Aqsa. In effect, they annexed the entire Mount. The official Al-Aqsa Mosque guidebook says.

> Al-Aqsa Mosque, also known as the Noble Sanctuary or Haram ash-Sharif, encloses thirty-five acres of fountains, gardens, paths, buildings and domes. At its southernmost end lies the large prayer hall often referred to as al-Aqsa Mosque, while at its centre lies the Dome of the Rock. The entire area, comprising nearly one sixth of the walled city of Jerusalem, is regarded as a mosque.

The entire Temple Mount, not just the structures, is now viewed as a place of worship.

THERE ARE VARIOUS STRUCTURES ON THE MOUNT

On the Temple Mount, or the Noble Sanctuary as Muslims call it, there are various structures including domes, prayer niches (mihrabs), fountains and arcades that decorate the area. In the course of time, the Temple Mount acquired a large number of fountains and small shrines as gifts. In the compound today, there are about 100 structures, both large and small.

THERE IS NO RESPECT FOR THE DOME OF THE ROCK

Though Muslims consider the entire Temple Mount to be sacred, when they pray facing Mecca, they do it with their backsides to the Dome of the Rock. Therefore, the lack of respect for the Dome is lacking every time there are Muslim prayers on the Mount.

THE DESTRUCTION OF JERUSALEM IS STILL REMEMBERED TODAY

While the Temple Mount is still in the hands of Muslims, the destruction of the Temple is still remembered in modern Jewish life. Louis Goldberg writes of the Passover Meal celebrated yearly by the Jews.

> There is the shank bone of a lamb, a memorial of the Passover Lamb. Prior to the destruction of the Temple, the main meat was the roasted lamb. The shank bone today is a mute testimony to the missing Temple. A roasted egg on the table also, as an emblem of mourning, inasmuch as the joys of the Temple service can no longer be experienced. The egg was not part of the seder [meal] prior to the destruction of the Temple.[5]

In many ways, and in many forms, the destruction of the Second Temple is continually remembered by observant Jews. All of this is in anticipation of the day when a new Temple will be built.

SUMMARY TO CHAPTER 15

In 1967, the city of Jerusalem was finally reunited under Israeli rule. The Temple Mount, however, remained in the hands of the Muslims. Efforts by a small number of Jews to pray on the Temple Mount have been frustrated by the police, the Muslims, and the government. This is in spite of the constitutional guarantees of freedom of worship in all Holy Sites. Because the government of Israel is basically secular, Jewish

---

5. Louis Goldberg, *Our Jewish Friends*, Chicago, Moody Press, 1977, p. 88

pressure for prayer on the Temple Mount comes from a minority of Israeli citizens.

For the Jews, the situation on the Temple Mount remains basically the same as it has been for the last two thousand years. They are without their Temple, and without the right to even pray publicly on their holiest site.

The current situation has kept the Temple Mount in the headlines since the time of Jerusalem's reunification. As we shall see, the Temple Mount will remain in the headlines because of its importance to "last days" Bible prophecy.

CHAPTER 16

Modern Preparations to Build the Third Temple

TO PERSONS OF THE JEWISH FAITH ALL OVER THE WORLD THE MILITARY VICTORY WON BY THE HEROIC MEN AND WOMEN AND CHILDREN OF ISRAEL UNDER MIRACULOUS CIRCUMSTANCES IS A GIFT OF GOD. THIS VICTORY WAS A SIGN BY OUR MAKER THAT NOW IS THE TIME TO REBUILD "THE TEMPLE OF GOD." GOD'S WILL WILL PREVAIL"

This was an advertisement that appeared in the *Washington Post* right after the capture of the Temple Mount in 1967.

We have seen the Jews have miraculously come back to their land after two thousand years of forced exile. Since 1967, the entire city of Jerusalem has been in their hands. As has been the case for the last 800 years, the Temple Mount, however, remains in the control of Muslims. This has greatly upset many Jews who saw the reunification of Jerusalem as a chance to build the Third Temple.

Although the Temple Mount remains in Muslim hands, this has not stopped a number of Jews from preparing for the next Temple. For the first time in 1,400 years, there is serious interest in rebuilding the Temple. We will now look at the current preparations to accomplish this task.

THERE HAS BEEN NO REAL CENTER FOR THE JEWISH PEOPLE

From the time of the destruction of the Second Temple, there has been no real center for the Jews. They have not been able to perform their religious duties as the Scriptures call for. The synagogues are not the same thing as the Temple. They are places of prayer, reading, and training. The priesthood has been inactive since Jerusalem's fall. This was predicted in Scripture. Indeed, we read about this in the Word of the Lord to the prophet Hosea.

> For the Israelites will live many days without king or prince, without sacrifice or sacred stones, without ephod or household gods (Hosea 3:4 NIV).

Since the retaking of the Temple Mount in 1967, there has begun an earnest attempt by some to prepare for the building of the Third Temple.

THE TALK OF TEMPLE REBUILDING

Immediately after the Israelis captured the Old City of Jerusalem, and the Temple Mount, there was talk of rebuilding the Temple. Hopes of rebuilding the Temple were also voiced among the Jewish people. For example, Rabbi Shlomo Goren said.

> From that time until the construction of the temple by Solomon, only one generation passed. So it will be with us.[1]

THIRD TEMPLE PREPARATIONS

Although the ban on visiting the Temple Mount remains in effect for Orthodox Jews, it has not stopped those in Israel from thinking about the realization of a long lost dream—the rebuilding of the Temple. Once the city of Jerusalem was retaken, this was no longer a pipe dream. Time magazine reports what is occurring.

---

1. Newsweek (October 20, 1990)

Since the destruction of Jerusalem by the Romans in A.D. 70, Conservative and Orthodox Jews have beseeched God four times a week to 'renew our days' as they once were—a plea for the restoration of the Temple. Although Zionism was largely a secular movement, one of its sources was the prayers of the Jews for a return to Palestine so that they could build a temple . . . Learned Jewish opinion has long debated when and how the temple can be rebuilt. The great medieval philosopher Maimonides, in his Code of Jewish Law, argued that every generation of Jews was obliged to rebuild the temple if its site was ever retaken, if a leader descended from David could be found, and if the enemies of Jerusalem were destroyed.[2]

Commenting on Isaiah 2:4, Rabbi Chaim Richman writes.

To witness the fulfillment of this ancient vision is a lifelong desire shared by all peoples—not only the Jews, who have longed through all their wanderings to return and rebuild Jerusalem from its ruins and to re-establish the Sanctuary of God in its midst.

The education of countless generations has been steeped in these verses. Isaiah's divine words formed the inspiration and driving force behind many diverse movements throughout world history, all of which centered around one purpose and objective: Jerusalem, the Holy City; Jerusalem, where the promised ultimate good shall be fulfilled; Jerusalem, which will once again be transformed into the spiritual center of all mankind.[3]

2. "Should the Temple be Rebuilt," *Time*, June 30, 1967
3. Chaim Richman, *The Odyssey Of The Third Temple*, Israel Publications And Productions, n.d., p. 63

WHY SHOULD THEY REBUILD THE TEMPLE?

The question arises as to the incentives the Jewish people would have for constructing a new Temple. For one thing, number 20 of the 613 commandments in the Torah (according to ancient Jewish sage Maimonides) calls for the building of a Temple in Jerusalem, if one does not exist, or orders the maintenance of a Temple, if it does exist.

Why would the Jews want to rebuild it? Two main reasons come to mind: (1) The fulfillment of a dream. (2) A rallying point for the nation.

REASON 1: THE FULFILLMENT OF A DREAM

The first incentive would be the fulfillment of a dream. For centuries the Jews did not possess their homeland—they were forced to wander as strangers and vagabonds across the face of the earth. Deep within their hearts, there has been a longing for the return to the land, and a rebuilding of the Temple.

The Temple is also a symbol of prosperity and a reminder of better days that the nation had. The desire for the restoration of the Temple has been the prayer of the Orthodox Jew since the destruction of the Second Temple in A.D. 70.

REASON 2: A UNIFYING FORCE FOR THE NATION

A rebuilt Temple could also be a unifying force for this small nation. During their relatively new existence as a reborn nation, Israel has experienced a series of major wars. A house of worship could serve as a rallying point for Jews worldwide. Furthermore, it could help unify the many Jewish factions that exist in Israel today.

The *Jerusalem Post* reported the following.

> The modern Jew found it difficult to face the binding obligation to rebuild the sanctuary, combined with the great dreams linked with it. He has suppressed the demands they make on him.

He was hesitant to use religious language to describe the historic return to Zion and to national sovereignty. There are indeed a few exceptions to this, as for example, 'the Third Temple,' once used by Ben-Gurion or the excessive use of prophetic terminology of the 'ingathering of the exiles' during the years of mass aliya.

Far beyond the formal commandment, the yearning to behold an actual concrete expression of a central religious and national focal point permeates all Jewish history.

Another argument is that the rebuilding as postulated by Maimonides requires a certain order of events: 1) coming to the land; 2) appointment of a king from the house of David; 3) blotting out the descendants of Amalek; and only then 4) the building of the Temple. The counter argument claims that, while this is indeed the ideal order of events, the events themselves are not necessary mutually interdependent and one must carry out whichever is possible at the time.[4]

Thus, the rebuilding of the Temple is considered central to Judaism. Chaim Richman expresses the thought of many contemporary Jews.

The eternal commandment to build the Holy Temple is alive and well in Jerusalem . . . waiting to be fulfilled by the Jewish people.[5]

MANY OF THE ACTIVISTS ARE MORE NATIONALISTIC THAN RELIGIOUS

It is interesting to note that some of the Temple Mount activists view the matter in more nationalistic than religious terms. Indeed, they see the Temple Mount as part of Israel, and until the Mount is in Israeli control, Israel does not have complete sovereignty over its country.

---

4. Pinchas H. Pell, "A Place For the Lord," *Jerusalem Post*, February 11, 1989
5. Chaim Richman, p. 63

One of their poets, Uri Zvi Greenberg, wrote, "Israel without the Mount—is not Israel. He who controls the Mount, controls the land of Israel."

CURRENT PREPARATIONS FOR A THIRD TEMPLE

For many years, preparations have been underway for its construction. However, there a number of issues which remain unresolved.

A PROBLEM: THE ASHES OF THE RED HEIFER

One of the problems with respect to the rebuilding of the Temple concerns the ritual defilement of the people. Since the Holy Land has been occupied by Gentiles, the Jewish people have become ritually defiled by contact with them. Some type of purification needs to occur before the Jews could enter the Temple Mount and begin rebuilding the Temple. This is especially true for those in the priesthood. The answer is found in the sacrifice of a red cow, or heifer.

IS IT A REQUIREMENT FOR THE THIRD TEMPLE?

Some insist that one of the requirements necessary for a Third Temple is the sprinkling of the ashes of a red heifer. In the past, the ashes of the red heifer were used to purify the people from defilement. The Book of Numbers records this command.

> The Lord spoke to Moses and Aaron: This is the ordinance of the law which the Lord has commanded: Instruct the Israelites to bring you a red heifer without blemish, which has no defect and has never carried a yoke. You must give it to Eleazar the priest so that he can take it outside the camp, and it must be slaughtered before him. Eleazar the priest is to take a some of its blood with his finger, and sprinkle some of the blood seven times directly in front of the tent of meeting (Numbers 19:1-4 NET).

THEY NEED AN UNDEFILED HEIFER

If it is necessary to sacrifice a red heifer to cleanse the people from ceremonial defilement, then a proper heifer must be found to accomplish this task. The heifer to be used in this sacrifice must meet certain requirements.

There are three different perspectives with respect to the sprinkling of the ashes of the red heifer to purify the priesthood before the building of the next Temple.

OPTION 1: FIND THE ORIGINAL ASHES OF THE RED HEIFER

Some believe the original ashes of the past red heifers need to be found. It is argued that red heifers were sacrificed seven times in the history of the Israel—from the time of the Tabernacle, to the time right before the Second Temple was destroyed. Each time a red heifer was sacrificed, its ashes were mixed together in an urn with the ashes of previously sacrificed red heifers. Therefore, these ashes must be found to assure the purity of the priesthood.

However, there is no biblical command for this to happen. Furthermore, it would be difficult, if not impossible to identify the buried ashes from previous sacrifices of red heifers. No one knows exactly where to look, for there are several possible sites listed in the historical records.

On a personal note: When the author had the honor of touring the Mount of Olives with Dr. Asher Kaufman (see Chapter 18) he pointed out a possible location for the burial of original ashes. Unfortunately, the owners of the property continually refused to allow any investigation of the site. Whether or not the original ashes were buried there is still a mystery.

OPTION 2: A NEW RED HEIFER IS TO BE SACRIFICED

A second line of thought is that there is no need to find the original ashes. One only needs to find a new red heifer that meets the requirements, and then sacrifice it.

OPTION 3: THERE IS NO SACRIFICE NEEDED

Finally, there are others who argue that no such sprinkling of the ashes of the red heifer is necessary for the rebuilding of the Temple, or the purification of the people.

SUMMARY TO THE RED HEIFER ISSUE

Sometime before the next Temple is built, there will seemingly be the sprinkling of the ashes of a sacrificed red heifer. These ashes will either be from those previously sacrificed, or more likely, from a newly sacrificed red heifer.

THE MENORAH

One of the main articles in the previous Temples was the Menorah, the Golden Lampstand. It is believed that the Menorah from the Second Temple may still exist. The *Jerusalem Post* reported the following.

> Religious affairs minister Shimon Shetreet who met with Pope John Paul II in Rome last week said he had asked for Vatican cooperation in locating the 60-kg. gold menorah from the Second Temple that was brought to Rome by Titus in 70 CE. Shetreet claimed that recent research at the University of Florence indicated the Menorah might be among the treasures in the Vatican's catacombs.[6]

The return of the Menorah from the Second Temple, if it still exists, would be a great incentive for the Jews to build their new Temple. It would be the only item that survived the destruction of the Second Temple. Again, we find that only time will tell whether or not the lost Temple Menorah still exists. If not, a newly constructed Menorah will be used.

----

6. Lisa Palmer-Billig, *Jerusalem Post*, International Edition, Week Ending January 27, 1996, p. 32

THE MODERN DAY SANHEDRIN

At the time of the construction of the next Temple, there will seemingly be a governing body, a Sanhedrin, in place. Interestingly, seventy-one rabbis have reconvened the Sanhedrin in Tiberias—the same city where this assembly last met.

This modern-day Sanhedrin, which is not recognized by every Orthodox Jew, has set a number of goals. For one thing, they are to locate the exact Temple site as well as build an altar on the Temple Mount. In addition, they are to locate descendants of the Davidic dynasty, which it supposedly has done, so as to reestablish the Jewish monarchy.

They believe that the legal stipulations that will govern Israel's relationship to the coming Temple and its services will also be under their charge. This is a further step in the preparation for a new Temple.

DNA AND THE NEW PRIESTHOOD

There has also been the recent discovery of a particular chromosome that links certain present day Jews from the family of Cohen back to Aaron, the first Great High Priest from the tribe of Levi. We read the following.

> The office of Cohen [priest] was granted to Aharon and his sons and to all their male progeny for all generations. The Torah states a number of times that the priesthood is an eternal covenant with the descendants of Aharon, the first Kohen, never to be lost.

> Molecular geneticists have recently discovered the "Cohen Modal Haplotype" which is a DNA signature consisting of specific genetic markers on the Y chromosome of the Cohens. This indicates a direct patrilineal descent of present day Kohanim from a single ancient ancestor, precisely as described in the Torah.

Explanations and implications are quoted as follows.

> The simplest, most straightforward explanation is that these men have the Y chromosome of Aharon. The study suggests that a 3,000-year-old tradition is correct, and has a biological counterpart.[7]

We also read.

> It's a beautiful example of how father to son transmission of two things, one genetic, one cultural, gives you the same picture.[8]

> For more than 90 percent of the Cohens to share the same genetic markers after such a period of time is a testament to the devotion of the wives of the Cohens over the years. Even a low rate of infidelity would have dramatically lowered the percentage.[9]

> Like first experiencing the Western Wall in Jerusalem, it's to me an extraordinary moving and intense experience of history and sacred history coming together. I think the Y chromosome research does the same thing genetically. It is a tangible embodied moment of connection to our past.[10]

Thus, it seems that there is a direct link of certain modern Jews with last name Cohen (Hebrew for priest) with the first high priest, Aaron. This is a further indication that the necessary requirements to build a new Temple are now in place.

---

7. Dr. Karl Skorecki, *New York Times*, January 7, 1997

8. Prof. Michael Hammer, *New York Times*, January 7, 1997

9. Dr. David Goldstein, Oxford University, *Science News*, October 3, 1998

10. L. Dorfman, San Francisco State University, *Science News*, October 3, 1998. From http://www.cohen-levi.org/ homepage

THE WORK OF THE TEMPLE INSTITUTE

As we mentioned in our introduction, one group that is making implements for the next Temple is the Temple Institute. It makes no secret of the fact that they hope to see the soon rebuilding of the Temple. The Temple Institute was founded to fulfill the biblical command to "build a Temple" insofar as it is now possible. The Institute points out that about one third of the 613 commandments according to Jewish sage Maimonides are dependent upon an actual Temple existing in Jerusalem.

In fact, the Temple Institute has spent years researching the materials, measurements, and the forms, of the 93 sacred vessels that are used in the Temple. They have begun construction of these vessels as well as the Priestly garments. These vessels are not mere items for display. Though they now serve as educational tools, it is the goal of the Temple Institute to use them when a Third Temple has been built. Randall Price explains.

> Since 1987, a group of rabbinical researchers, designers, and craftsmen under the direction of Rabbi Yisrael Ariel founded the Temple Institute in the Jewish Quarter of Jerusalem. Creating what they call a "Temple-in-waiting," their efforts have produced detailed blueprints for the Third Temple and ritually qualified vessels, garments, and other items necessary for a restoration of the Temple services. Among these items is the apparel for the High Priest: his eight-layered woven robe, the golden crown worn on his head, and his jeweled breastplate bearing the names of the tribes of Israel. Other items include the blue-purple dye (tchelet) for the tsitsit of the priests robes, the eleven sacrificial incense spices, urns, ewers, incense pans, forks, shovels, and carts (for burnt offerings). In addition, the gold and silver mizrak (vessels used to dispense sacrificial blood on the altar), the golden laver, flasks, and measuring cups (used in the libation offerings).

They also created plans for the vessels for the meal offerings, the lottery boxes (for the Day of Atonement), the mortal and pestle, and the stone vessel (kelal) for grinding and holding the purifying ashes of the red heifer. The also have plans for the golden menorah (lampstand) and cleaning instruments and oil pitchers for replenishing the oil for its light, the Table of Showbread, the Altar of Incense, the silver trumpets (for assembling Israel at the Temple), and the barley altar. These utensils and furniture for the Temple have been prepared with the intent of utilizing them in the rebuilt Temple in the near future.[11]

The group is indeed preparing for the Third Temple. In a brochure they have produced, the Temple Institute states its aims.

> The dream of the Temple is as old as the Jewish people itself. Even on the Red Sea, only minutes after G-d's miraculous salvation of Israel, Moses raises his voice in song: "You will bring them and plant them on the mountain of your inheritance, the place where you have set for your dwelling, O L-rd, the Temple of God which your hands have established. . ."

> The hope for the rebuilding of the Temple was born on the very day of its destruction almost 2,000 years ago. Rabbi Akiva comforted his weeping colleagues by proclaiming that if the prophecies of destruction have come to pass, the fulfillment of the prophecy of redemption and rebuilding is certainly to follow. In the course of 2,000 years, the Jewish people have never forgotten the Temple. On our holidays we pray: "Build your house as at the first, set your Temple on its foundations, allow us to see it built and make us joyous in its establishment, return Priests to their service and Levites

---

11. Randall Price, *Rose Guide To The Temple*, Rose Publishing Inc., Torrance, California, 2012

to their songs and music, and return Israel to their pleasant places, and there we will ascend and be seen and bow down before you. . ." On our days of mourning we cry: "It would be a delight to my soul to walk naked and barefoot upon the desolate ruins of your Holy courts, in place of your Ark which has been hidden . . ." At our most joyous we break a glass to remember its destruction.

The dream of rebuilding the temple spans 50 generations of Jews, five continents and innumerable seas and oceans. The prayer for the rebuilding is recited in as many languages as are known to humanity. These prayers are recited in prisons and ghettos, study halls and synagogues, homes and fields everyday for 2,000 years of exile, in the face of poverty and persecution and seemingly hopeless peril, now gain a new dimension with the return of the people of Israel to the Land of Israel, with the rebirth of the Jewish state and the creation of a Jewish army and the flowering of the desert and the scientific and social strides made by the nation of Israel. This new dimension is: a Possibility.[12]

MODERN TECHNOLOGY EMPLOYED

The Temple Institute receives visitors and conducts tours. In the exhibition hall, some of the implements for the Third Temple are on display. The Institute is a blend of the old and the new. To research these ancient implements, modern technology is used—including the most advanced computer programs.

THE ODYSSEY OF THE THIRD TEMPLE

The Temple Institute has produced a number of books including one titled *Odyssey Of the Third Temple*. The book focuses upon the need for a future Temple, as well as the process for its rebuilding. The

12. Chaim Richman, *The Odyssey Of The Third Temple*, Israel Publications And Productions, n.d., p. 65

following extracts from the book reveals the importance they attach to the rebuilding of the Temple.

> Seven things were contemplated (By the Holy One, Blessed be He) before creation: Torah, Repentance, the Garden of Eden and Gehinnom, the Throne of Glory, the Holy Temple and the Messiah's identity

> The Holy Temple appears in this divine cosmic plan precisely because it represents the apex of human longing: The ability for man to engage in a direct relationship with God. The world awaits the day when the Temple in Jerusalem will once again be the global center of spiritual values. At this one spot of Earth, unlike any other, it will be revealed that "God is One and His Name is One (Zechariah 14:9).[13]

THE JEWISH HOPE: A NEW TEMPLE

Since the destruction of the Second Temple in A.D. 70, it has been the desire of the Jewish people to see a Third Temple built. Rabbi Leibel Reznick sums up their feelings.

> The Holy Temple was the very heart and soul of the Jewish people. Before the First Temple was ever built, King David longed for it. In anticipation, he dedicated his royal treasures to the Temple building. He composed Psalms, liturgical works to be sung in the Temple service.

> After the Second Temple was destroyed, Jews yearned to rebuild it. It is now almost 2,000 years since the destruction of the Temple and still, three times each day, Jews express in their prayers their hopes for the rebuilding of their Temple. The Temple is not only a proud memory of the past, but represents the future of the Jewish nation.

---

13. Chaim Richman, *The Odyssey Of The Third Temple*, Israel Publications And Productions, n.d., p. 65, 68

The future Temple, according to prophetic visions, will herald an era when no nation will raise up a sword against another, when war will not be taught, and when instruments of battle will be beaten into plowshares. The Jewish Temple is the hope of mankind. The future Temple will be God's palace on earth. God shall reign as King and His subjects will be at peace with one another.[14]

MAKE THE DREAM COME TRUE

The Temple Institute sells a picture of modern day Jerusalem and the Temple Mount. The picture has airbrushed out the two Islamic Holy Places—The Dome of the Rock and the Al Aksa Mosque. In its place is an artist's conception of the Third Temple placed upon the Temple Mount in present-day Jerusalem. A sign underneath in Hebrew and English reads: "Make the dream come true."

IT WILL BE A NIGHTMARE!

The Third Temple will indeed be built in modern day Jerusalem on the Temple Mount, but as we shall see, it will not be a dream—it will be an absolute nightmare. In fact, the Third Temple will be the center stage for the worst disaster ever for the Jewish people.

SUMMARY TO CHAPTER 16

Today the Temple Mount remains in turmoil. As certain groups are preparing to build a Third Temple, government forces in Israel, as well as the Muslim powers that be, are keeping this from occurring. The secular Jews do not care, and many of the Orthodox Jews believe that the Third Temple will have to await the arrival of the Messiah.

Will the next Temple be built? Yes, the Bible says so.

---

14. Leibel Reznick, *The Holy Temple Revisited*, Northvale, New Jersey: Jason Aronson, Inc., 1990

CHAPTER 17

A Missing Piece of the Temple Puzzle: The Lost Ark of the Covenant

"The Ark of the Covenant is more than archaeology"

Indiana Jones in *Raiders of the Lost Ark*

The stage is set for the construction of the Third Temple. As we have seen, the Jews are back in their land, and are controlling all of Jerusalem, yet the authority of the Temple Mount is in the hands of the Muslims. We have also noted that there is a group of people making the implements to be used in a soon-to-be-built Temple.

There is, however, one article that they will not rebuild, and that may, or may not, play a part in this final "last days" drama. That object is the long lost Ark of the Covenant.

THE REASON FOR THE CONSTRUCTION OF THE TABERNACLE AND TEMPLE: THE ARK

As we have emphasized, the original reason for the construction of the Tabernacle, and later the Temple, was a place to house the Ark. All the articles of furniture were built in reference to the Ark. There was no purpose for either structure without the Ark of the Covenant.

The last biblical mention of the Ark is 2 Chronicles 35:3 where it was placed back into the Temple in the realm of King Josiah—shortly before the destruction of the Second Temple. We read.

He [Josiah] said to the Levites, who instructed all Israel and who had been consecrated to the LORD: "Put the sacred ark in the temple that Solomon son of David king of Israel built. It is not to be carried about on your shoulders. Now serve the LORD your God and his people Israel" (2 Chronicles 35:3 NIV).

After that time there is only silence with regard to its fate.

THERE WAS NO ARK IN JESUS' DAY

We have also seen that the Second Temple, the one in Jesus' day, did not have the Ark of the Covenant in the Holy of Holies. In addition, there is no concrete evidence today that the Ark still exists or that someone has it, though there are many theories as to its possible location.

IN SEARCH OF THE LOST ARK

We have written a book that thoroughly documents the history of the Ark of the Covenant, and the different possibilities as to what happened to it (*In Search of The Lost Ark: The Quest For The Ark of The Covenant*). We will briefly summarize the various ideas as to the possible fate of the Ark.

OPTION 1: THE ARK MAY BE FOREVER LOST

It is possible that the Ark was destroyed sometime in the distant past. If this is what happened, then it most likely occurred when the Babylonians destroyed the city of Jerusalem and the first Temple in 587 B.C.

OPTION 2: WAS IT TAKEN BY FOREIGN INVADERS?

There have been those who attacked Jerusalem in the past who could have taken the Ark of the Covenant. The various possibilities include: The Egyptians, the Northern Kingdom of Israel, the Babylonians, and the Romans. Of these, the only one that is biblically possible is the

Babylonians. The Ark of the Covenant still existed in 621 B.C. when Josiah had it placed back in the Temple (2 Chronicles 35:3). This is *after* the invasion of the Egyptians, and the Northern Kingdom of Israel.

After the Babylonian captivity (536 B.C.) the Ark was missing. Since it was not in the Second Temple, it could not have been taken by the Romans when they destroyed the city in A.D. 70. If some foreign invader had taken away the Ark, then it would have had to have been the Babylonians.

OPTION 3: WAS THE ARK HIDDEN?

There are a great number of people who believe the Ark was hidden at some time in the past, waiting to be discovered in the "last days." The question that no one has to the answer to is, "Where was the Ark hidden?"

There are a number of possible theories as to the location of the Ark of the Covenant. The most popular include: Mount Nebo in Jordan, Qumran, or under the Temple Mount. There is also a bizarre theory that the Ark was taken to Ethiopia in the 10th century B.C., but there is no evidence for this whatsoever.

IS IT UNDER THE TEMPLE MOUNT?

If the Ark has been hidden, waiting to be discovered in the "last days," the most probable spot would be somewhere under the Temple Mount in Jerusalem. It is possible that the Ark of the Covenant has been hidden for over 2,600 years, directly below the place where Solomon's Temple stood. There have been reports that the Holy Ark been discovered in a secret passageway underneath the Temple Mount.

SOLOMON'S HIDING PLACE

It has been theorized that when King Solomon built the Temple, he also ordered a secret underground vault to be built to hide the Ark of the Covenant. If Jerusalem were ever put to siege by foreign invaders, the Ark could then be taken from the Holy of Holies and placed into this hiding place. Though the Bible does not speak of such a secret room many Jewish authorities have argued for its existence.

WAS IT PLACED THERE DURING JOSIAH'S REIGN?

This underground hiding place was supposedly put to use in the reign of King Josiah. We have already seen that Josiah ordered the Ark returned to the Temple after it had been previously removed.

> He [Josiah] said to the Levites, who instructed all Israel and who had been consecrated to the LORD: "Put the sacred ark in the temple that Solomon son of David king of Israel built. It is not to be carried about on your shoulders. Now serve the LORD your God and his people Israel" (2 Chronicles 35:3 NIV).

Many Jewish interpreters speculate that Josiah did not put the Ark back in the Holy of Holies at this time, but rather placed it in Solomon's secret hiding place.

HE KNEW THE TEMPLE WOULD BE PLUNDERED

He did this because he knew the treasures of the Temple were about to be plundered. King Josiah had been told by Huldah the Prophetess that the Temple would be destroyed soon after his death. We read.

> Hilkiah the priest, Ahikam, Akbor, Shaphan and Asaiah went to speak to the prophet Huldah, who was the wife of Shallum son of Tikvah, the son of Harhas, keeper of the wardrobe. She lived in Jerusalem, in the New Quarter. She said to them, "This is what the LORD, the God of Israel, says: Tell the man who sent you to me, 'This is what the LORD says: I am going to bring disaster on this place and its people, according to everything written in the book the king

of Judah has read. Because they have forsaken me and burned incense to other gods and aroused my anger by all the idols their hands have made, my anger will burn against this place and will not be quenched.' Tell the king of Judah, who sent you to inquire of the LORD, 'This is what the LORD, the God of Israel, says concerning the words you heard: Because your heart was responsive and you humbled yourself before the LORD when you heard what I have spoken against this place and its people—that they would become a curse and be laid waste—and because you tore your robes and wept in my presence, I also have heard you, declares the LORD. Therefore I will gather you to your ancestors, and you will be buried in peace. Your eyes will not see all the disaster I am going to bring on this place' (2 Kings 22: 14-20 NIV).

Knowing of this impending destruction, Josiah ordered the Ark to be put in this secret underground vault. Many Rabbinical interpreters believe that the Ark has remained hidden in that place ever since and shall only be manifested and brought out again in the days of the Messiah.

WAS IT HIDDEN BY AN ANGEL?

There is also the tradition that an angel hid the Ark. According to one Jewish apocryphal source called *The Vision of Baruch*. Baruch, the scribe of Jeremiah, saw an angel take the Ark and hide it beneath the sealed foundation stone on the Temple Mount known as the "Well of Souls."

The angel then spoke to the earth saying, "hear the word of God and receive what I commit to your care until the last times."

JEREMIAH MAY HAVE HIDDEN THE ARK

It has also been taught that the prophet Jeremiah hid the Ark before the destruction of the Temple. Rabbi Leibel Reznick writes.

Before the destruction of the First Temple . . . the prophet Jeremiah hid the national treasures of the Jews under the Holy Temple to prevent them from falling in the hands of the invading Nebuchadnezzar and his Babylonian troops. The treasures included the Holy Ark, the Two Tablets with the Ten Commandments carved upon them, the staff of Aaron, the oil for anointing compounded by Moses, and a container holding the last sample of the manna that sustained the Children of Israel during their forty years of wandering through the desert. After the seventy years of the Babylonian exile, the Jews returned to Zion, but, alas, the treasures were never found.[1]

IS THE ARK BURIED UNDER THE CHAMBER OF WOOD?

According to a late Jewish tradition, the Ark was buried under the Chamber of Wood in the Temple prior to the destruction of the First Temple. Leibel Reznick writes.

The Mishnah (Shekalim 6:1) records that the Holy Ark was hidden in a secret passageway that began beneath the Chamber of Wood, which was located in the northwestern corner of the Women's Courtyard . . . there is an underground room . . . in that corner. It is a chamber forty-four feet below ground level, and has a vaulted ceiling. It has never been explored.[2]

PRESENTLY NO ONE CAN INVESTIGATE

Could any of these places contain the lost Ark? There are several things keeping interested parties from thoroughly investigating these claims. First, it is impossible to do any excavating from the top of the

---

1. Leibel Reznick, *The Holy Temple Revisited*, Northvale, New Jersey: Jason Aronson, Inc., 1990

2. Reznick, p. 127

the sacred vessels of the Temple could be hidden in case of approaching danger. In this regard, Midrashic and Talmudic tradition teach that King Josiah of Israel, who lived about forty years before the destruction, commanded the Levites to hide the Ark of the Testimony, together with the menorah, the anointing oil and other items in this secret hiding place which Solomon had prepared.[3]

WHERE THE ARK FITS IN

It is possible that the Ark will never be found, and a Third Temple could still be built without it. We have already seen that the Ark of the Covenant was not in the Second Temple—which lasted from 515 B.C. to A.D. 70. Likewise, a Third Temple could be constructed without the Ark.

The discovery of the Ark, however, could speed up this process of the Temple's rebuilding by giving the Jews an incentive to begin. In fact, if the Ark is discovered, it may not be possible to stop the building of a Third Temple. Indeed, many Jewish authorities in the past have spoken of the day when the Ark will be discovered, and the Third Temple built.

IT WOULD BE NECESSARY TO BUILD THE TEMPLE IF THE ARK WERE FOUND

One Israeli Rabbi put it this way.

> If we find the ark, it will force us to build the temple. After all the first temple was built to house the ark of the covenant. If we find the ark, what would we do with it? We couldn't store it in the prime minister's basement. It would demand the rebuilding of the temple. However, if we find the ark or not we are going to build the temple of Almighty God on the . . . temple mountain.

---

3. *Jerusalem Post*, International Edition, week ending May 21, 1992, p. 23

According to one Jewish tradition, when the Messiah comes he will perform seven miracles to prove his authenticity, one of them is discovering the location of the Ark of the Covenant. Only time will tell, however, if the lost Ark will be found and placed in the Third Temple.

SUMMARY TO CHAPTER 17

We are not certain if the long lost Ark of the Covenant still exists. Since its disappearance over 2,600 years ago there have been various theories as to what happened to this sacred object. However, no one really knows for certain.

If it is found, the Ark of the Covenant would undoubtedly play a central role in the next Temple. The Temple, however, will be rebuilt, with or without the Ark, because the Scripture demands it.

It is still not certain that the Ark of the Covenant will ever be found. It may not exist any longer. There are, however, more formidable obstacles that are keeping the Jews from building their next Temple. Our next chapter will look at those obstacles.

CHAPTER 18

Two Major Obstacles:
Where and How to Build the Next Temple

No other place in the world has inspired such zealous activity for over 3,000 years. No other place in the world has had so much written about it—barbs of ridicule as well as songs of praise. No other place in the world has been so closely studied and scrutinized as Jerusalem, so that hardly a month goes by without at least one research paper being published on one aspect or another of the Temple Mount. Nevertheless, despite all that has been written and done, a multitude of secrets still lay hidden in the belly of the earth.[1]

For the Muslims the history of the Mount began with Muhammad's vision of his night's journey from Mecca to Jerusalem and thence with a spring, that left a mark, much revered, on the surface of the . . . Temple Mount, up to heaven. Over the spot, the present "Dome of the Rock" was built, everything lying beneath it being, to the Muslim, irrelevant, even the insights of archaeology in the last hundred years, even the result of contemporary excavations being conducted now. Even these, to the descendants of the Muslims who walled up the historical underground passages and kept "infidels" and curious away, are unimportant.[2]

---

1. *Encyclopedia Judaica*, vol. 6, pp. 113,114

2. Gaaylah Cornfield, *The Mystery of the Temple Mount*, Jerusalem: Barak Israel Guidebook Publishers, Ltd., n.d., pp. 9-10

The preparations are presently being made for the construction of the Third Temple. There are, however, major obstacles to keep those from accomplishing this task.

TWO MAJOR PROBLEMS FACE THE JEWS

The first problem concerns where to build the Temple. There is no agreement as to the exact site of where the Temple stood.

Assuming the precise site is determined, there is even a more formidable obstacle in the way—how will the Muslim's allow a new Temple to be built upon their sacred site?

We can make the following observations about these two problems.

PROBLEM 1: WHERE TO BUILD THE NEXT TEMPLE

When the city of Jerusalem was reunited by the Jews in 1967 much speculation arose concerning the rebuilding of the Temple. According to Scripture, the only place the Temple could be built is the city of Jerusalem. The Lord has said.

> But now I have chosen Jerusalem for my Name to be there, and I have chosen David to rule my people Israel (2 Chronicles 6:6 NIV).

THE SITE MUST BE CORRECTLY IDENTIFIED

Furthermore, in order to build the Third Temple, the *precise* location of the former Temples in the city of Jerusalem must be correctly identified. There are a number of reasons for this.

First, the exact site for the First Temple was divinely chosen by the Lord.

> So the Lord's messenger told Gad to instruct David to go up and build an altar for the Lord on the threshing floor of Ornan the Jebusite (1 Chronicles 21:18 NET).

In addition, there was a continuity between the previous Temples which have been built. In fact, each one was constructed with its Holy of Holies enclosing the same stone on Mt. Moriah. This is known in Hebrew as Even ha-Shetiyah—"The Foundation Stone."

It was upon this very stone that the Ark of the Covenant had been set and where the Shekinah Glory, God's Divine Presence, had descended from heaven at the dedication of the First Temple. The Bible says.

> Once the priests left the holy place, a cloud filled the Lord's temple. The priests could not carry out their duties because of the cloud; the Lord's glory filled his temple (1 Kings 8:10,11 NET).

Later, during the time of Ezekiel, we find that the glory of the Lord departed from the Holy Temple.

> Then I perceived that the glory of the God of Israel was there, as in the vision I had seen earlier in the valley. . . Then the cherubim spread their wings with their wheels alongside them while the glory of the God of Israel hovered above them. The glory of the Lord rose up from within the city and stopped over the mountain east of it (Ezekiel 8:4; 11:22,23 NET).

The good news is that the Lord has promised that His glory would someday return to a future Temple.

> Then he brought me to the gate that faced toward the east. I saw the glory of the God of Israel coming from the east; the sound was like that of rushing water; and the earth radiated his glory. It was like the vision I saw when he came to destroy the city, and the vision I saw by the Kebar River. I threw myself face down. The glory of the Lord came into the temple by way of the gate that faces east. Then a wind lifted me up and brought me to the inner court; I watched the glory of the Lord filling the temple (Ezekiel 43:1-5 NET).

In sum, there is no other legitimate place for the building of the next Temple. Indeed, it must be on the exact site as the previous two Temples.

NOTHING HAS SURVIVED FROM THE SECOND TEMPLE

However, nothing that would lead us to the exact location of the Second Temple has been found to the present time. Archaeologists have not discovered any trace of the walls, gates, or furniture. This has not stopped them from wanting to know where the Temple originally stood.

> About one hundred fifty years ago the famous Jerusalem explorer Charles Warren declared, "We want to know where the Temple was."[3]

The same question is still being asked today. Where was the Temple located?

> More recently archaeologist Kathleen Kenyon wrote, "Absolutely nothing survives of the temple built by Herod".[4]

The famous authority on ancient Jerusalem, M. Avi-Yonah, agreed.

> We know little more about the Temple Mount than Warren did a century ago. The location of the actual Temple, the central problem, cannot yet be ascertained.[5]

Since the Temple Mount is presently under Muslim control, any on site work to determine where the Temple had once stood is simply impossible. The Muslims, for their part, do not even acknowledge there ever was a Jewish Temple located on the Temple Mount.

---

3. Charles Warren, Extracts from the report of the public meeting of the Palestine Exploration Fund, on June 11, 1868, p. 6

4. Kathleen Kenyon, *Digging Up Jerusalem*, London, 1974

5. M. Avi-Yonah, "Jerusalem of the Second Temple Period," in *Jerusalem Revealed*, The Israel Exploration Society and Shikmona, Jerusalem, 1975, p. 13

The fact that archaeological excavation on the Temple Mount is not possible has not stopped scholars from attempting to locate the Temple site through other means.

THERE ARE A NUMBER OF POSSIBLE LOCATIONS AS TO WHERE THE TEMPLE STOOD

There have been various theories as to where the ancient Temple stood. They include the following popular ones.

1. The Temple stood over the site of the Dome of the Rock Shrine. The sacred rock was where the Holy of Holies was located.

2. Another view says that the sacred rock was where the altar of sacrifice stood; not the Holy of Holies. The altar was located slightest east of the Temple proper. Therefore, the Temple would have stood slightly west of the Dome of the Rock.

3. The Temple stood 106 meters to the north and the west of the Dome of the Rock shrine. A small monument known as the "Dome of the Spirits" or the "Dome of the Tablets" stands today where the Holy of Holies once stood.

4. The Temple originally stood to the south of the Dome of the Rock— between it and the Al Aksa Mosque. A large fountain stands today where the Holy of Holies once stood.

5. Another recent theory says the Temple originally stood even further to south of the Dome of the Rock, near the Al Aksa Mosque.

6. One other theory, which has not gained much prominence, is that the present-day Temple Mount is not the site of the Temple. The Temple was actually built hundreds of yards to the south of the Dome of the Rock in the ancient city of David.

We can summarize them in the following manner.

OPTION 1: THE TEMPLE STOOD OVER THE PRESENT-DAY DOME OF THE ROCK

The most generally accepted view among scholars is that the Dome of the Rock shrine was built over the location of the First and Second Temple. The Dome was built over a rock-mass known to the Muslims as *as-Sakhra*. This rock-mass, where it is thought that the Holy of Holies was located, is the highest point on the Temple Mount. Because it is believed that this golden Dome was purposely erected over this rock-mass to keep the Jews from ever building another Temple, the site of the Dome of the Rock has been a popular choice for the original location of the Temple.

OPTION 2: THE TEMPLE STOOD WEST OF THE DOME OF THE ROCK

Another possibility is that the Temple stood west of the sacred rock. The Jewish Encyclopedia notes.

> The most probable site of the Temple is just west of the "Dome of the Rock" in the center of the Mosque of Omar. The bronze altar was probably built upon this rock. The mosque was built over a rock the traditions of which are sacred; probably the site was the same as that of the temple which Hadrian erected to Jupiter. This in turn was the site of Herod's temple, which would naturally be that of Solomon's. The persistency of sacred sites in the East makes this most likely.[6]

According to this theory, the sacred rock was the where the altar of sacrifice stood—not the Holy of Holies. This would place the location of the Temple a little to the west of the Dome.

WHAT WAS THE ROCK?

As we have just noted, there is disagreement among those who propose the Dome of the Rock site as to where the Holy of Holies stood. Some

---

6. *Encyclopedia Judaica*, p. 139

believe the rock-mass marks the spot of the Holy of Holies. Others believe the Holy of Holies was further west on the Temple Mount. The rock-mass was where the altar of sacrifice stood.

Each of these theories asserts that the "sacred rock" was an integral part of the First and Second Temple. In recent years, the Dutch architect, Leen Ritmeyer, has made a solid case for the Dome of the Rock site as the original location for the Temple with the sacred rock as the location for the "Holy of Holies." As mentioned, this is the generally accepted view of where the ancient Temples stood.

OPTION 3: THE THEORY OF ASHER KAUFMAN: THE DOME OF THE TABLETS

There is another theory as to where the Temple had originally stood— one that has been proposed by a plasma physicist, and an observant Jew, the late Dr. Asher Kaufman. In 1974, Kaufman began to explore the subject of the original location of the Temple.

Being an observant Jew he faced an immediate problem. According to Jewish Law, no observant Jew is allowed to walk on the Temple Mount for fear he might accidentally walk upon the Holy of Holies. This rule seemed to keep Dr. Kaufman from making a first-hand examination of the Mount. However, he discovered that a non-priest could walk upon the area if he were considered to be cleaning, repairing, or rebuilding the Temple. Though the rebuilding for him was purely theoretical, this allowed him to walk upon the Temple Mount and do his research.

THE APPROACH OF KAUFMAN

Kaufman's approach combined a number of methods. These included the study of ancient Jewish sources that describe the Temple, and its vicinity, along with the Temple rituals. He also applied techniques from modern methods of measurement, astronomical observations, as well as onsite inspection. In 1977, Kaufman wrote.

> An air of mystery surrounds the Second Temple in Jerusalem. Where was it situated in the Temple area (Haram

ash-Sharif)? What did it look like? For generations, scholars in general, clergy, archaeologists, engineers and historians have attempted to answer these two questions. The rock as-Sakhra in the Dome of the Rock plays a central role in the vast majority of these deliberations. It is regarded as the site either of the Holy of Holies or of the Altar of Sacrifice. A third question—is there any visible sign of the Temple today?—was answered by Simons (1952, p. 435) in the negative: "In contrast, however, with the principal monument of ancient Athens the buildings within the sacred precincts at Jerusalem have utterly disappeared."

THE TEMPLE WAS IN A DIFFERENT LOCATION THAN USUALLY BELIEVED

Dr. Kaufman's research led him to a startling conclusion—the site of the Temple is not the Dome of the Rock! According to Kaufman, the Temple's original location was 330 feet to the north and the west of the Dome. The site has a small shrine, or cupola, known as the "Dome of the Spirits" or "Dome of the Tablets." He believed that the flat rock, which this small shrine covers, was the location of the Holy of Holies—where the Ark of the Covenant stood. He wrote.

> It is almost axiomatic among scholars that no trace of the Jewish Temple is to be found on Jerusalem's Temple Mount. . . Despite this scholarly consensus, there are, however, traces of remains—a line of stones, a worked rock-mass, a cistern—and these ancient relics are sufficient, when added to the literary sources to locate the Second Temple, and even to trace out the First Temple, on the Temple Mount.

> One of the most surprising conclusions from this evidence is that the golden Dome of the Rock in the middle of the Temple Mount was not built on the site of the Temple but to

the south of it. The Original Temple site is approximately 330 feet (100 meters) to the northwest of the Dome of the Rock.[7]

THE DOME OF THE SPIRITS

Kaufman believed that the title of this small shrine may be a reminder of its original purpose. He wrote the following.

> In Arabic this cupola is called Qubbat el-Arwah, Dome of the Spirits. Has this Arabic name preserved an ancient memory of the holiness of the site? In Sinai, where the glory of the Lord appeared before the whole community of Israel, Moses and Aaron addressed the Lord as "God of the spirits of all mankind" (Numbers 16:22; see also Numbers 27:16, Ezekiel 37, Job 12:10). Dome of the Spirits is certainly an appropriate name to mark the dwelling place of the Lord's name, the center of his Divine presence.[8]

The biblical basis for this name, the Dome of the Spirits, is possibly found in two passages in the Old Testament Book of Numbers. We read these words.

> But Moses and Aaron fell facedown and cried out, "O God, God of every human spirit, will you be angry with the entire assembly when only one man sins?" . . . May the LORD, the God of every human spirit, appoint someone over this community (Numbers 16:22; 27:16 NIV).

THE DOME OF THE TABLETS

The shrine has another name, the Dome of the Tablets. Kaufman noted its significance.

7. Asher S. Kaufman, "Where The Ancient Temple of Jerusalem Stood," *Biblical Archeological Review*, Vol. IX No. 2, March/April 1983, p. 42

8. Kaufman, *Biblical Archeological Review*, p. 45

But this cupola has another Arabic name: Qubbat el-Alouah, Dome of the Tablets. In the Holy of Holies of Solomon's Temple was kept the Ark of the Covenant, now lost, containing the two stone Tablets of the law given to Moses on Mount Sinai. According to M. de Vogue, the name Dome of the Tablets was given to this cupola because it is dedicated to the memory of the Tablets of the Law. Once more a name preserves the ancient memory of the location of the Holy of Holies.[9]

Kaufman traced the tradition regarding the Dome of the Tablets back to the seventh century A.D. Some Christians, Jews, and Muslims have accepted his view as the actual site of the Temple. However, his theory has been rejected by other scholars and archaeologists. Again, only time will tell whether or not this was the original site.

On a personal note: The author became good friends with Asher Kaufman and had the privilege of touring the Temple Mount, as well as the Mount of Olives, with this wonderful and brilliant man. I'll be forever thankful for hours we spent discussing the location of the Temple.

OPTION 4: SOUTH OF THE DOME

A fourth possibility is that the Temple stood on the southern side of the Temple Mount. This would place it between the two later structures built upon the Mount—the Dome of the Rock Shrine and the Al Aqsa Mosque. The *Jewish Encyclopedia*, though noting that people in the past have argued for a southern location of the Temple, dismisses the theory.

There can be no doubt that the Temple of Solomon was situated upon the more easterly of the two hills which form the present Haram area in Jerusalem, in the center of which is

---

9. Kaufman, *Biblical Archeological Review*, p. 45

the Mosque of Omar. Ferguson, Trupp, Lewin and W.R. Smith held that the Temple was built in the southwest corner of the present Haram area: but this view is false. That site is a part of an artificial extension of the level of the Temple area over the Tyropeon valley and probably was not made before the time of Herod.[10]

However, there have been some recently discovered facts that may provide evidence that the Temple did stand on the southern part of the Mount. Israeli architect Tuvia Sagiv has presented a case for the southerly location. However, as with the case of Asher Kaufman's "northern hypothesis," not everyone is convinced by his evidence.

OPTION 5: THE TEMPLE STOOD FURTHER SOUTH ON THE MOUNT

Similar to the previous option, is a new theory that claims the Temple stood even further to the south of the Dome of the Rock—at the site of the Al Aksa Mosque rather than between these two structures. Only time will tell if this theory gains any traction among the experts.

OPTION 6: IT WAS NOT BUILT ON THE TEMPLE MOUNT

This is also the theory of the late Bible scholar Ernest Martin. He concluded that scholars have made wrong conclusions with respect to the site of the ancient Temple. His view is that the Temple was located some one thousand feet down from the present-day Mount in the area of the ancient City of David. The problem is that this theory has never gained any traction with qualified scholars.

ONLY TIME WILL TELL AS TO WHERE THE TEMPLE STOOD

This is a brief summary of some of the more popular theories which have been proposed as to where the Temple originally stood. In fact, about twenty different sites on the Temple Mount have been suggested

10. *Encyclopedia Judaica* p. 114

for the exact location of the Temple. It would take an entire book to examine the arguments for each site, pro and con. Only time will tell which theory is correct since it is presently impossible to do any excavating on the Mount.

However, locating the original Temple is not the only problem that the Jews face.

PROBLEM 2: HOW CAN THE TEMPLE BE BUILT?

The second problem, assuming the correct site of the Temple is known, concerns how they are going to build the Third Temple. How could the Jews construct a Temple upon the third most sacred spot of Islam? There have been, at least, five proposed solutions. They are as follows.

SOLUTION 1: THE DOME WILL BE DESTROYED

One possible solution is the destruction of the Dome of the Rock. When Israel became a recognized state in 1948, Rabbi Levy, of the Tremount Temple of New York, said: "The Temple of Jerusalem will be rebuilt . . . It is more than possible that the very religious will insist on tearing down the Mosque and erecting a Temple much like Solomon's."

The leader of the Temple Mount Faithful, Gershon Salomon, has said, "I'm sorry but the Mosque must be moved."

THE POSSIBLE REACTION

It is hard to image what would happen if the Jews undertook to demolish the Dome of the Rock, and replace it with a Temple. Destroying sacred Muslim buildings upon the Temple Mount would be an invitation for the destruction of Israel. It is unthinkable that the government of Israel would allow anything like this.

A NATURAL DISASTER?

It is possible that some natural disaster will occur that will destroy the Dome of the Rock. This could be an earthquake, underground explosion, or some other natural disaster. When asked how is it possible that the Temple be built with the Dome of the Rock standing over its location historian Israel Eldad said.

> It is, of course, an open question. Who knows? Perhaps there will be an earthquake.[11]

It has also been suggested that perhaps an errant missile may destroy the Dome.

The obvious problem with this view is that the Muslim world would immediately want the Dome rebuilt, if it were destroyed—either accidentally, or on purpose.

SOLUTION 2: THE JEWS PURCHASE THE TEMPLE MOUNT

There is also the possibility that the Dome of the Rock could be bought. Jews, in times past, have offered to buy the Temple Mount. Shortly after the Six Day War in 1967, a letter came to the Muslim Council in Jerusalem from a substantial Jewish organization in the United States offering to buy the Temple Mount, with the Al Aqsa Mosque and the Dome of the Rock. The price offered was 100 million dollars. The Muslims told them it was not for sale.

SOLUTION 3: INCORPORATE THE TEMPLE WITH EXISTING STRUCTURES

Others have suggested a joint project, with Muslims and Jews working together on the Temple Mount. They would put aside their differences and build a Third Temple together, as a monument to peace.

Aryeh Kotzer, principal of a school of religion in Israel, has published a booklet in which he maintains that the Dome of the Rock could simply be incorporated into the Third Temple.

The example of the Tomb of the Patriarchs in Hebron (the Machpelah), where Jews and Muslims worship together side by side, is cited as how

---

11. Israel Eldad. "Should the Temple Be Rebuilt" *Time*, June 30, 1967, p. 56

these two faiths could worship together. However, the idea of this type of co-existence was dealt a considerable setback with the massacre of twenty-nine Muslims at the Tomb of the Patriarchs in February 1994.

In light of history, this suggestion seems impossible, but stranger things have been known to happen.

SOLUTION 4: BUILD AT A DIFFERENT SITE IN JERUSALEM

Some have suggested that the Third Temple be built on a different site in the city of Jerusalem. If the theory of Ernest Martin proves to be correct then the Dome would *not* have to be destroyed or incorporated into the next Temple. This would seemingly solve a lot of problems while creating another set of problems.

However, if the present Temple Mount is indeed the site of the Temple, as almost everyone agrees that it is, then we are faced with the same problem of how to build it on a Muslim holy site.

It must be emphasized that other sites, apart from the location of the original Temple, will not suffice. The Bible commands that the Temple be built upon the exact site that God chose. The Bible says in the Book of Deuteronomy.

> But you are to seek the place the LORD your God will choose from among all your tribes to put his Name there for his dwelling. To that place you must go . . . Offer them only at the place the LORD will choose in one of your tribes, and there observe everything I command you (Deuteronomy 12:5,14 NIV).

God chose the site. Consequently, the Temple must be built there.

The Jews acknowledge this fact.

> The exact location of the altar is extremely precise, and can never be changed . . . and it is a universally accepted tradition that the place on which David and Solomon built the

altar (on the site of the threshing floor of Aravnah) is the same spot on which Abraham built the altar upon which he bound Isaac . . . this is the same spot on which Noah built an altar upon leaving the ark, and this is the altar upon which Cain and Abel offered their sacrifices, and upon which Adam offered his sacrifice: And from that very place Adam was created. The sages said: 'Adam was created from the very spot that atones for him'.[12]

To sum up, the idea that the Temple could be built on another location, apart from the original site, has no real merit. If the Temple could have been built on another site, then it already would have built. Lack of materials or funds is not what is stopping the building process. The process is being stopped because the site is unavailable—assuming the Dome of the Rock is the exact location of the past Temples.

SOLUTION 5: THE ACTUAL TEMPLE SITE IS NOT THE DOME OF THE ROCK

A final possibility is that the Temple could be built elsewhere on the Mount. We have mentioned two alternative theories as to the location of the Temple. If either proves to be correct, then a Third Temple could be built without removing either the Dome of the Rock or the Al Aqsa Mosque. It would also solve the age-old question as to how the Temple could be built upon the Mount without causing a "holy war." If the Dome of the Rock does not have to be removed, then theoretically a Third Temple could be built adjacent to it.

THE ACCOUNT IN REVELATION CHAPTER 11 MAY SUPPORT THIS IDEA

Apparently the Third Temple could conceivably be built without disturbing the Dome of the Rock. The Dome of the Rock would be presently sitting in what was the "outer court" of the Temple.

---

12. Chaim Richman, *The Odyssey Of The Third Temple*, Israel Publications And Productions, n.d., p. 12

If that turns out to be the case, then it would conform precisely to a vision given to the Apostle John in the Book of Revelation. John, apparently transported forward through time, was given a vision of the Temple Mount. He wrote.

> I was given a reed like a measuring rod and was told, "Go and measure the temple of God and the altar, with its worshipers. But exclude the outer court; do not measure it, because it has been given to the Gentiles. They will trample on the holy city for 42 months" (Revelation 11:1,2 NIV).

In this passage, the word used for Temple is naos—the Temple proper, exclusive of the courts. The reference to the outer court—the court of the Gentiles—is strange in that it should be singled out. John was told not to measure it because it had been given over to the "nations" or "Gentiles." This may suggest that the Third Temple will be built without disturbing the Dome of the Rock, or the Al Aksa Mosque.

IS THIS AN IMPOSSIBLE TASK?

There are many who deny this could happen. Since the Muslims consider the entire Temple Mount as a mosque, it is unlikely that they would allow a Third Temple to be built on their holy ground. To Islam, it would be an abomination, an affront to their God, Allah. A Temple, built side by side to the Dome of the Rock, would be impossible for many to conceive.

In addition, Muslim theology claims that land once owned by Islam is forever holy to them and must be repossessed if lost. This makes the Temple Mount theirs forever.

THE JEWISH OBJECTION: IT IS THE "HOLY" TEMPLE

Furthermore, many Jews scoff at the idea of a Temple built in the back-yard of the Dome of the Rock. What kind of glorious Temple would this be, they ask? The Jews would have to share the sacred space with their longtime enemies. They believe that it would be an outrage architecturally, aesthetically and historically. Their answer continues to be "remove the Dome."

Again we note the theory of Ernest Martin. If it proves to be correct then the Dome of the Rock and the present Temple Mount can remain intact with a Third Temple built south of that location. However, the so-called evidence for this theory is not convincing to scholars.

THE MYSTERY WILL BE SOLVED SOME DAY

Right now the exact location of the ancient Temple is a mystery. However, we know that one day this mystery will definitely be solved but it will only happen according to *God's* timetable.

SUMMARY TO CHAPTER 18

Two major things are keeping the Third Temple from being constructed. First, there is no consensus of opinion as to where the Temple originally stood. Before the Third Temple can be built, the correct site has to be determined. Current conditions make it impossible to do the right type of excavation, or study, to determine the original Temple site. Once it is possible to excavate or study the area, the site of the Temple can be determined.

However, a more formidable problem concerns the permission to build a Temple. This is seemingly impossible—given the present situation between the Jews and Muslims.

Yet, according to Scripture, these obstacles will be overcome and the Third Temple will be built. We will now consider what the Scripture has to say with regard to a future Temple.

PART 3

The Coming
Temple

Our last section will take us into the future. What does the Bible have to say regarding the future of the Jews, the holy city of Jerusalem, and the Temple Mount? What role will they play in end-time events?

CHAPTER 19

The Third Temple: The Anticipation of Scripture and Ancient Bible Commentators

Don't let anyone deceive you in any way, for [that day will not come] until the rebellion occurs and the man of lawlessness is revealed, the man doomed to destruction. He will oppose and will exalt himself over everything that is called God or is worshiped, so that he sets himself up in God's temple, proclaiming himself to be God.

2 Thessalonians 2:3,4

We have seen the promise and fulfillment of the Jews returning back to their ancient homeland. We have also seen the prediction and fulfillment of the unification of Jerusalem. Today the Temple Mount remains a source of turmoil between Jews and Muslims. Preparations are being made for the building of the Temple, but with the Muslims in control of the Temple Mount, such preparations seem futile. What will happen next? Does the Bible have anything to say about the matter?

The Bible does indeed predict another Temple will be built on the Temple Mount. Not only has it been predicted by Scripture, it has also been predicted by Bible commentators of the last two thousand years— those who have literally believed the prophecies of the Scripture.

THE TESTIMONY OF SCRIPTURE

In both the Old and New Testament, we find the anticipation of the construction of another Temple that is yet to be built. Contrary to the previous Temples, this Temple will *not* be blessed by God, because it will be built in unbelief of Him and His Word.

We can make the following observations as to what the Scripture has to say with respect to a future Temple.

THE ABOMINATION OF DESOLATION (MATTHEW 24:15)

In the last week of His life, Jesus pronounced judgment upon the city of Jerusalem and the Temple with the following words.

> Jerusalem, Jerusalem, you who kill the prophets and stone those sent to you, how often I have longed to gather your children together, as a hen gathers her chicks under her wings, and you were not willing. Look, your house is left to you desolate. For I tell you, you will not see me again until you say, 'Blessed is he who comes in the name of the Lord' (Matthew 23:37-39 NIV).

This must have confused Jesus' disciples because they had come to believe that Jesus was the promised Messiah. In fact, just a few day previous on Palm Sunday, Jesus acknowledged that He was the Christ.

> As he was drawing near—already on the way down the Mount of Olives—the whole multitude of his disciples began to rejoice and praise God with a loud voice for all the mighty works that they had seen, saying, "Blessed is the King who comes in the name of the Lord! Peace in heaven and glory in the highest!" And some of the Pharisees in the crowd said to him, "Teacher, rebuke your disciples." He answered, "I tell you, if these were silent, the very stones would cry out" (Luke 21: 37-40 ESV).

In addition, Isaiah 2:1-4 tells us that the Messiah will rule from the Temple in Jerusalem.

> This is what Isaiah son of Amoz saw concerning Judah and Jerusalem: In the last days the mountain of the LORD's temple will be established as the highest of the mountains; it will be exalted above the hills, and all nations will stream to it. Many peoples will come and say, "Come, let us go up to the mountain of the LORD, to the temple of the God of Jacob. He will teach us his ways, so that we may walk in his paths." The law will go out from Zion, the word of the LORD from Jerusalem. He will judge between the nations and will settle disputes for many peoples. They will beat their swords into plowshares and their spears into pruning hooks. Nation will not take up sword against nation, nor will they train for war anymore (Isaiah 2:1-4 NIV).

Jesus acknowledged that He is the promised Messiah, and Scripture says that the Messiah will rule from the Temple in the city of Jerusalem. But now He is talking about the destruction of the Temple. How can this be?

We then find the disciples calling attention to the buildings.

> As Jesus left the temple courtyard and was walking away, his disciples came to him. They proudly pointed out to him the temple buildings. Jesus said to them, "You see all these buildings, don't you? I can guarantee this truth: Not one of these stones will be left on top of another. Each one will be torn down" (Matthew 24:1-2 God's Word).

This must have really confused them. Consequently, after they walked from the Temple Mount to the Mount of Olives they had some questions that needed to be answered.

> As Jesus was sitting on the Mount of Olives, the disciples came to him privately. "Tell us," they said, "when will this

happen, and what will be the sign of your coming and of the end of the age (Matthew 24:3 NIV).

Jesus spoke of the Temple being desolated. Consequently, the disciples wanted a specific sign of His coming. He said the following. Jesus gave them the answer.

> So when you see the abomination of desolation spoken of by the prophet Daniel, standing in the holy place (let the reader understand), then let those who are in Judea flee to the mountains. Let the one who is on the housetop not go down to take what is in his house, and let the one who is in the field not turn back to take his cloak. And alas for women who are pregnant and for those who are nursing infants in those days! Pray that your flight may not be in winter or on a Sabbath. For then there will be great tribulation, such as has not been from the beginning of the world until now, no, and never will be. And if those days had not been cut short, no human being would be saved. But for the sake of the elect those days will be cut short (Matthew 24:15-22 ESV).

Jesus spoke of the "abomination of desolation" as *the* sign that would signal the period of "great tribulation." We can make the following conclusions from His Words.

1. Jesus was asked for a *specific* sign regarding His return. He gave a definite sign—the abomination of desolation. In other words, He considered Daniel's prophecy as something which was yet to be fulfilled at some time in the future.

2. The abomination of desolation concerns the Temple and its services. The phrase "Holy Place" is a technical term for the Temple.

3. He referred His listeners to the Prophet Daniel who, on four occasions, speaks of a defiling of the Temple.

4. It is important to realize that Jesus' prophecy was *not* fulfilled with the literal destruction of Jerusalem in A.D. 70. The abomination of desolation has *not yet* occurred.

5. Therefore, the sign of His return revolves around a functioning Temple. Since there is no Temple presently standing, the logical conclusion is that another Temple needs to be built.

THE MAN OF SIN SITS IN THE TEMPLE OF GOD (2 THESSALONIANS 2:3,4)

Another passage of Scripture that anticipates a future Temple is found in Paul's second letter to the Thessalonians. We read.

> Don't let anyone deceive you in any way, for that day will not come until the rebellion occurs and the man of lawlessness is revealed, the man doomed to destruction. He will oppose and will exalt himself over everything that is called God or is worshiped, so that he sets himself up in God's temple, proclaiming himself to be God (2 Thessalonians 2:3,4 NIV).

Several things from this passage add to our knowledge of these future events.

1. Before Jesus Christ returns, there will be a person coming on the scene of history known as the "Man of Sin." He is the "final Antichrist."

2. This man had not yet appeared at the time of Paul's' writing to the Thessalonians (around A.D. 50).

3. The identity of this "man of sin" will be known when he performs an act of abomination in the Temple. He will actually claim to be God while in the Temple itself.

4. This act defines what Jesus referred to as the "abomination of desolation."

5. From the time of Paul's writing, until the destruction of the Second Temple, this event did *not* occur.

6. For this event to occur in the future, another Temple needs to be built.

THE FALSE PROPHET WILL GIVE LIFE TO THE IMAGE OF THE FINAL ANTICHRIST (REVELATION 13:11-15)

The final Antichrist has a cohort known as the "second beast" or the "false prophet." This false prophet gives life to an image of the beast causing the inhabitants of the earth to worship the beast, and his image. The Bible says.

> Then I saw another beast, coming out of the earth. It had two horns like a lamb, but it spoke like a dragon. It exercised all the authority of the first beast on its behalf, and made the earth and its inhabitants worship the first beast, whose fatal wound had been healed. And it performed great signs, even causing fire to come down from heaven to the earth in full view of everyone. Because of the signs it was given power to perform on behalf of the first beast, it deceived the inhabitants of the earth. It ordered them to set up an image in honor of the beast who was wounded by the sword and yet lived. It was given power to give breath to the image of the first beast, so that it could speak and cause all who refused to worship the image to be killed (Revelation 13:11-15 NIV).

From this passage we learn more things about the final Antichrist and the coming Temple.

1. This incident further illustrates Paul's words in Thessalonians about the "abomination which causes desolation." The next Temple is defiled by this man of sin by declaring to be God and having his image placed in the Holy of Holies.

2. Consequently, we need not restrict Paul's words to the physical presence of the final Antichrist himself in the Temple. It is an image of the Antichrist that is erected there, and commands the worship of the

people. Those who do not worship him or his image will be put to death. In other words, this act of abomination will cause desolation. Therefore, Jesus' reference to the abomination of desolation is fully illuminated by what John says as recorded in the Book of Revelation.

3. This is another indication that another Temple needs to be built since the erection of an image of the final Antichrist has never occurred in history.

THE COMMAND TO MEASURE THE TEMPLE (REVELATION 11:1,2)

A final passage in the New Testament that speaks of a future Temple is also found in the Book of Revelation. It reads as follows.

> I was given a reed like a measuring rod and was told, "Go and measure the temple of God and the altar, with its worshipers. But exclude the outer court; do not measure it, because it has been given to the Gentiles. They will trample on the holy city for 42 months" (Revelation 11:1,2 NIV).

John is told to measure the Temple. He must be referring to a future Temple for the following reasons.

1. It is generally agreed among scholars that John wrote the Book of Revelation at the end of his life (around A.D. 90). If this be the case, then he had to be referring to a Temple that was to be built in the future, for the Second Temple was destroyed in A.D. 70.

2. Even if Revelation was composed before the destruction of the Second Temple, chapter 11 refers to events that are still future. Indeed, the surrounding events of the measuring of the Temple in verses 1 and 2 (the appearance of the two witnesses, the existence of the man of sin, the death and resurrection of these two witnesses, the great earthquake in Jerusalem, and the appearance of the Ark of the Covenant in heaven) are still future. None of these predicted events have happened yet. Hence, the Temple John was told to measure is *yet* to be built.

THE OLD TESTAMENT

This scenario fits well with certain passages in the Old Testament which speak of a Temple that is dishonored. Indeed, there are four passages in the Old Testament, three in the Book of Daniel and one in Isaiah that speak of the defiling of a future Temple.

PASSAGE 1: SOMEONE WILL CONFIRM A COVENANT (DANIEL 9:27)

The prophet was told the time that this would happen. We read elsewhere in Daniel.

> He will confirm a covenant with many for one 'seven.' In the middle of the 'seven' he will put an end to sacrifice and offering. And at the temple he will set up an abomination that causes desolation, until the end that is decreed is poured out on him (Daniel 9:27 NIV).

This passage tells us the following.

1. The coming man of sin will make a covenant with the Jewish people for seven years. Evidently this will involve the building of the Temple, and the right to begin their sacrifices.

2. In the middle of the seven-year period, after three and one half years, this final Antichrist will break the covenant with Israel. He will order the sacrifices stopped, and will desecrate the Temple. This act is known as the "abomination of desolation." The desolation will consist of the attempted annihilation of the Jewish people.

PASSAGE 2: THE SANCTUARY IS DEFILED (DANIEL 11:31)

A second passage is found in Daniel which speaks of a future defiling of the Temple.

> His armed forces will rise up to desecrate the temple fortress and will abolish the daily sacrifice. Then they will set up the abomination that causes desolation (Daniel 11:31 NIV).

From this particular verse we learn the following.

1. The Temple will be defiled by a future leader and his armed forces.

2. The daily sacrifice will be abolished.

3. An abomination will be put in place of the daily sacrifices.

4. These acts will cause desolation to Jewish people.

While this passage was initially fulfilled by Antiochus IV, it would prefigure the actions of the final Antichrist actions (see Daniel 9:27; 12:11). In 167 B.C., Antiochus did away with the regular sacrifice and committed an abomination that caused desolation to the Jewish people. He dedicated the holy Temple to the god Zeus and offered a pig on its altar. Antiochus also slaughtered a number of Jews.

The apocryphal book of First Maccabees uses the same term Greek phrase "the abomination of desolation" or "desolation sacrilege" to describe this event.

> Now on the fifteenth day of Chislev, in the one hundred forty-fifth year, they erected a desolating sacrilege on the altar of burnt offering. They also built altars in the surrounding towns of Judah (1 Maccabees 1:54 NRSV).

This further indicates that this phrase "the abomination of desolation" was well-known to the Jews in Jesus day, as well as exactly what the phrase meant—the desecration of the Temple.

PASSAGE 3: THERE IS A PRECISE TIME LIMIT FOR THE RULE OF THE ANTICHRIST (DANIEL 12:5-7,11)

After these events occur, we find that there is a limited time this final Antichrist will rule. Once more we read from the writings of the prophet Daniel.

I, Daniel, watched as two others stood there, one on each side of the river. One said to the man clothed in linen who was above the waters of the river, "When will the end of these wondrous events occur?" Then I heard the man clothed in linen who was over the waters of the river as he raised both his right and left hands to the sky and made an oath by the one who lives forever. It is for a time, times, and half a time. Then, when the power of the one who shatters the holy people has been exhausted, all these things will be finished … From the time that the daily sacrifice is removed and the abomination that causes desolation is set in place, there are 1,290 days (Daniel 12:5-7,11 NET).

We learn the following from these verses.

1. This passage again tells us that the daily sacrifice will be taken away.

2. In addition, it is reiterated that an abomination that causes desolation is placed in the Temple.

3. These events will be the work of the future Antichrist.

4. The time frame in which this man of sin will rule is very specific. It is 1290 days, or time, times and half a time—three and one half years. His power will then be shattered.

5. Once this time period has been completed, the kingdom of God will come to the earth!

PASSAGE 4: THERE ARE UNACCEPTABLE SACRIFICES OFFERED (ISAIAH 66:1-4)

The prophet Isaiah seems to have been speaking of the Third Temple when he recorded God saying.

This is what the LORD says: "Heaven is my throne, and the earth is my footstool. Where is the house you will build for me? Where will my resting place be? Has not my hand made all these things, and so they came into being?" declares the LORD. These are the ones I look on with favor: those who are humble and contrite in spirit, and who tremble at my word. But whoever sacrifices a bull is like one who kills a human being, and whoever offers a lamb is like one who breaks a dog's neck; whoever makes a grain offering is like one who presents pig's blood, and whoever burns memorial incense is like one who worships an idol. They have chosen their own ways, and they delight in their abominations; so I also will choose harsh treatment for them and will bring on them what they dread. For when I called, no one answered, when I spoke, no one listened. They did evil in my sight and chose what displeases me (Isaiah 66:1-4 NIV).

Isaiah's passage tells us the following.

1. The Temple built by the Jews will not be honoring to God.

2. This passage stresses there is no need for the people to build a house for God. The Temple is no longer necessary in the plan of God.

SUMMARY OF THE BIBLICAL TEACHING

We can summarize what the Bible says about a future Temple as follows. There are certain events that are predicted which assume the Jews will control Jerusalem and the Temple Mount. These events include the forced stopping of the Temple sacrifices, and the defiling of the Holy of Holies. For these events to occur as prophesied a new Temple must be built and functioning. There is no reason whatsoever to understand these predictions in a figurative or symbolic sense. Indeed, the next Temple is coming! Scripture demands it.

THE TESTIMONY OF BIBLE COMMENTATORS

The idea that a Third Temple will be built by the Jews, in unbelief of Jesus, is not something new to our day. In fact, since the destruction of the Second Temple there have been Bible commentators who have predicted this event. We will give only a small sampling of what these Bible teachers have said.

Irenaeus (A.D. 140-202) wrote that Antichrist would sit in a rebuilt Jerusalem Temple.

> He will reign a time, times, and half a time (Daniel 7:25) i.e. three and a half years and will sit in the temple at Jerusalem; then the Lord shall come from heaven and cast him into the lake of fire, and shall bring to the saints the time of reigning, the seventh day of hallowed rest, and give to Abraham the promised inheritance.[1]

The early Christian writer, Hippolytus (A.D. 220), wrote.

> Which horn (Daniel 7) shows that the one which budded is none other than the Antichrist who will restore the kingdom of the Jews . . . Christ Jesus sprung from the Hebrews; He too will be born a Jew. Christ declared His flesh to be a temple and raised it on the third day, so he (the Antichrist) will restore at Jerusalem the Temple of Stone.

Cyril of Jerusalem, writing in A.D. 360, stated the following.

> Antichrist sits in the temple of God. But what temple is spoken on? The Jewish temple. . . If he came to the Jews as the Messiah, he would surely wish to be worshipped by the Jews, that he may deceive them as much as possible.

We also find the same types of predictions in the last few centuries. In 1861, Robert Govett wrote.

> The temple in Jerusalem will be yet rebuilt by the Jews in unbelief, and be the scene of wickedness greater than has ever

---

1. Irenaeus, *Against Heresies*, Book V, Chapter 30, Paragraph 4

appeared . . . While, then, the temple had been destroyed at the date of the writing of Revelation [approximately A.D. 90], it was hereby predicted that it would be rebuilt . . . Till the Jew is brought back to his own land, and the temple and sacrifices restored, the prophetic part of the Apocalypse does not begin.[2]

The list goes on and on. Clearly, many Christians, for the last 2000 years, have taught that a Third Temple will be built before the Lord returns to the earth and sets up His everlasting kingdom.

WHAT SHOULD WE EXPECT TO SEE BASED UPON WHAT THE BIBLE PREDICTS?

When we examine everything that the Scripture has to say about the Jews, Jerusalem, and the coming Temple, we can make a number of observations as to what we should expect to see in the future. The key is what we read about in the Book of Daniel. Daniel 12:11 tells us that once the daily sacrifice has been removed, and the abomination that causes desolation takes place, it is 1,290 days until the kingdom of God comes to the earth.

> From the time that the daily sacrifice is removed and the abomination that causes desolation is set in place, there are 1,290 days (Daniel 12:11 NIV).

NINE THINGS MUST BE IN PLACE

For these events to literally occur, there must be at least nine things in place. They include the following.

1. The Jews Must Still Exist In The Last Days

2. They Have Returned To Their Ancient Homeland

---

2. Robert Govett, *Govett on Revelation*, Volume I, Miami Springs, Florida, 1981, reprint of originally published in London in 1861 titled *The Apocalypse: Expounded by Scripture*. p. 497

3. They Are An Actual Nation/State

4. Their Territory Includes East Jerusalem: The Temple Mount

5. They Are In Their Land In Unbelief Of Jesus

6. They Have A Functioning Temple

7. The Temple Is Built On The Same Site The Previous Temples Stood

8: Israel Has Authority Over The Temple Mount

9. The Sacrifices Are Taking Place

Each of these nine things must be in place before this event can happen.

We will consider them one at a time.

ASSUMPTION 1: THE JEWS MUST STILL EXIST IN THE LAST DAYS

The Scripture assumes that the Jews will still exist in the "last days." In fact, the Bible contains numerous references of the Jews existing at the time of the end. For example, we read the following in the Book of Daniel.

> At that time Michael, the great prince who protects your people, will arise. There will be a time of distress such as has not happened from the beginning of nations until then. But at that time your people—everyone whose name is found written in the book—will be delivered (Daniel 12:1 NIV).

Daniel's people, the Jews, will still exist when the "last days" arrive.

ASSUMPTION 2: THEY HAVE RETURNED TO THEIR ANCIENT HOMELAND

Not only will these descendants of Abraham, Isaac, and Jacob still exist, they will return to their ancient homeland. Indeed, we read about what the Lord says to Gog; a man who will lead a "last days" attack upon the nation of Israel.

A long time from now you will be called into action. In the distant future you will swoop down on the land of Israel, which will be enjoying peace after recovering from war and after its people have returned from many lands to the mountains of Israel (Ezekiel 38:8 NIV).

In the "last days," the "distant future," the Jewish nation will have returned to their ancient homeland from many countries. Among other things, Scripture also says that the land of Israel will have recovered from the devastation of war.

ASSUMPTION 3: THEY ARE AN ACTUAL NATION/STATE

These returning Jews will have formed a modern state. In other words, they will be a recognized political entity with a governing body, a military and a land with specific borders.

ASSUMPTION 4: THEIR TERRITORY INCLUDES EAST JERUSALEM: THE TEMPLE MOUNT

The nation of Israel will be in control of East Jerusalem where the Temple Mount stands. Indeed, to build a Temple on the Temple Mount they must have control of this geographic area.

As we have already noted, in 1948, when Israel became a modern state, East Jerusalem and the Temple Mount were not under their control. In fact, the city of Jerusalem was divided in half with the Temple Mount under the control of Transjordan. Careful Bible students predicted there would have to be another war in which the Israelis would capture East Jerusalem and the Temple Mount. This took place in 1967—the Six Day War. The city was now united.

ASSUMPTION 5: THEY ARE IN THEIR LAND IN UNBELIEF OF JESUS

At this time, as a nation, they will be in unbelief of Jesus as their Messiah. Indeed, the fact that they will build a Temple shows that the people have not accepted the sacrifice which Jesus made upon the cross. The Temple and its sacrifices pointed to the coming of the Messiah and His death. Once Jesus died for the sins of the world the Temple was no longer necessary. Hence, constructing a Temple is a denial of Jesus as the Christ.

Please note that each of these five assumptions of Scripture are in place. There are four that remain unfulfilled before the stopping of the sacrifices, and the abomination of desolation, can take place.

ASSUMPTION 6: THEY HAVE A FUNCTIONING TEMPLE

This one is rather obvious. To offer sacrifices there must be a Third Temple that is built and functioning. As we have previously mentioned, preparations are now being made for this to happen.

ASSUMPTION 7: THE TEMPLE IS BUILT ON THE SAME SITE THE PREVIOUS TEMPLES STOOD

This means the original location of the Temple will be discovered. As we have emphasized, there is only one place in which the Jews can build the Third Temple—the exact location where the previous Temples had stood. Someday that location will be discovered.

ASSUMPTION 8: ISRAEL HAS AUTHORITY OVER THE TEMPLE MOUNT

Not only does the territory of Israel include East Jerusalem, the nation must have authority over the Temple Mount. The Temple Mount today, though in the territory of Israel, is under the control of Islam. According to Scripture, that will change someday.

ASSUMPTION 9: THE SACRIFICES ARE TAKING PLACE

Finally, to stop the sacrifices, it is assumed that they have already started. For this to happen, the previous eight assumptions, that we have just considered, must all be in place.

In sum, nine things must be in place for the sacrifices in the Temple to be stopped and the abomination of desolation to occur. Miraculously, five of them have been literally fulfilled. The preparations are now being made for these final four things to take place. As always, the predictions made in the Bible, the Word of God, come true!

SUMMARY TO CHAPTER 19

From the time the Romans destroyed their last Temple two thousand years ago, the building of a new Temple has been the hope of the Jews. Furthermore, the next Temple is predicted and anticipated by both testaments. The final drama before Jesus Christ returns has this future Temple at center stage.

In addition, many Bible interpreters, from the second century onward, have predicted the return of the Jews, and the rebuilding of the Temple.

However, the Bible predicts that this new Temple will eventually be defiled. Indeed, Scripture says that the sacrifices will be stopped and something abominable will be placed in the Holy of Holies.

As we have observed, for all these things to occur at least nine things must be set in place. This includes the Jews still exist, they are back in their ancient homeland, they have formed a modern state, the entire city of Jerusalem is under their control, and the nation is in unbelief of Jesus. These five things are presently in place.

This sets the stage for the next Temple to be built and the sacrifices to start. However, before this takes place, the exact location of the previous Temples must be known and the Israelis must have full authority over the Temple Mount.

It is only a matter of time before this occurs.

CHAPTER 20

The False Messiah
And the Temple of Doom

I have come in my Father's name, and you do not accept me;
but if someone else comes in his own name, you will accept
him.

Jesus (John 5:43)

The preparations are now being made to build the Third Temple.
However, the seemingly insurmountable obstacle, which stands in the
way, is that the Temple Mount is presently in control of the Muslims.
Islam considers the Temple Mount to be the third holiest site in their
religion, and have no plans to allow the Jews to build anything, let
alone a Temple, upon their sacred ground. Yet the Bible says a Third
Temple will be built. If the Bible says so, then it will indeed happen.

How can this dilemma be solved? To the Jews, the person who will
solve this problem will be their promised Messiah.

JEWISH EXPECTATIONS OF THE MESSIAH

The rabbinical view is the Messiah is not the divine "Son of God" as
Christians believe. He will be a man, not God. He will be a combina-
tion of an Elijah, Solomon and David. Aviezer Ravitsky, professor of
Jewish thought at the Hebrew University writes.

For two millennia . . . Jews have prayed for a redemption involving returning to their land in a Messianic era. In some views, the Messiah would lead this process, in others his arrival would be the culmination of the process. Israel would then live in perfect peace with the rest of the world—swords into plowshares.[1]

Rabbi Shlomo Riskin writes.

In Maimonides magnum opus Mishneh Torah, we are given a clear cut description of the Messiah's role, how are we to identify him, and what will life be like during the "days of the Messiah."

Simply stated, the Messiah (or anointed king/leader) will be a flesh and blood head of state who, in a perfectly natural way, will usher in a period of peace for the world.

The Messiah will rebuild the Temple. He will gather in the exiles. He will keep the commandments. We are warned that we shouldn't expect a person who performs miracles or raises the dead. Nor should we think that in the days of the Messiah there will be a change in the order of creation. The only difference between our world and the [world in the] days of Messiah is that the Jews won't be enslaved to the rest of the nations," writes Maimonides.

Maimonides makes it clear that these concepts are derived from the Bible . . . He sees Redemption as a historical promise. But the conditions set forth are that the Jews must return, physically and spiritually to the Land and to Tora.

This gives one Jewish perspective of the coming Messiah.

---

1. *Jerusalem Post*, International Edition Week Ending March 12, 1994, p. 7

FOR THE JEWS, THE MESSIAH IS LINKED WITH THE NEXT TEMPLE

Therefore, the identity of the Messiah is linked with the rebuilding of the Temple. The Jews are not looking for God to become a human, or even looking for a miracle-working man—they are looking for someone who will bring peace to the world through the Temple in Jerusalem.

While Christians believe the Messiah has already come, Judaism is waiting for his arrival. One Jewish leader said.

> They believe that once the Temple is built, Jesus will come again. We expect the Messiah to come for the first time. Let's build the Temple, and see what he looks like.

WHO WILL BUILD THE THIRD TEMPLE?

Part of the many controversies regarding a Third Temple revolves around *how* it will come about. There are two basic options about how the new Temple will be constructed: one view is that the people here on earth will construct it. A second viewpoint is that it will supernaturally descend from heaven. This issue has been a source of debate amongst the Jews.

OPTION 1: IT CAN BE BUILT BEFORE THE MESSIAH ARRIVES

Some believe it could be built before the Messiah arrives. The Jewish sage Maimonides taught this. One Jewish writer explained it this way.

> As Maimonides writes in his classic Letter on Religious Persecution, "Not one of any of the commandments of the Torah is dependent upon the Messiah's arrival." Based upon this understanding it stands to reason that a situation could arise wherein a third Temple could be built in Jerusalem and the messiah has still not yet arrived. This concurs with the opinion expressed in the Jerusalem Talmud: "The [third] Holy Temple will in the future be re-established before the establishment of the Kingdom of David."

From this perspective, the Messiah will not necessarily be involved in the rebuilding of the Temple.

OPTION 2: THE MESSIAH WILL BUILD THE TEMPLE

There are, however, many Jews who expect the Messiah to be the one who builds the Third Temple. They are not concerned with the preparations for a new Temple, because they do not believe it is their responsibility. Consequently, they do not get involved in issues such as freedom of worship on the Temple Mount, or any of the other matters that the aforementioned groups have dedicated themselves to dealing with.

PRESENTLY THERE ARE THESE TWO DIFFERENT PERSPECTIVES

Therefore, we have two different streams of thought among the Jews: one group believes it is *their* responsibility to do as much as possible to make preparations for the Third Temple. Those who follow the teachings of the Jewish sage Maimonides believe it is up to them to have all the preparations ready and then build the Third Temple when circumstances permit.

A second group believes the building of the next Temple will be entirely the work of the Messiah. This was the teaching of the Jewish sage Rashi. Those holding this perspective will wait for the Messiah to come. In other words, he will do the work of rebuilding the Temple.

Both groups, however, expect the Messiah to come and a Third Temple to be built. Still, there is the present-day problem of the Muslims and how to build the Temple on their sacred site.

THE SOLUTION TO THE PROBLEM: THE COMING WORLD RULER

The seemingly insoluble problems with the Temple Mount, the Muslims, and the building of the Temple, will be solved by a future world ruler. The Bible says that a man will arise on the world scene who is unlike anyone before or since. This man will apparently have all the answers to the world's problems. He will bring a false peace to the world. In addition, he will, most likely, aid the Jews in the building of their Temple and the re-institution of their sacrificial system.

This will possibly cause them to accept him as their Messiah, or, if he is a Gentile, they may assume that the Messiah will immediately come after this Third Temple has been built with his help.

JESUS' PREDICTION

According to Jesus, this coming world leader will be received by Israel. He said.

> I have come in my Father's name, and you do not accept me; but if someone else comes in his own name, you will accept him (John 5:43 NIV).

While the nation rejected Jesus, they will receive this man.

THE FINAL ANTICHRIST—THE COMING CAESAR

This world ruler, who is to come, is known by a number of names in Scripture—the most popular being the "Antichrist." The term Antichrist is made up of two Greek words *anti* which means, "in the place of," or "instead of," and *Christ* which is the "anointed one" or "Messiah." Consequently, the Antichrist is a person who attempts to take the rightful place of the true Messiah.

The Bible teaches that many antichrists will arise throughout the course of the present age. Jesus said.

> For many will come in my name, claiming, 'I am the Messiah,' and will deceive many. . . and many false prophets will appear and deceive many people. . . At that time if anyone says to you, 'Look, here is the Messiah!' or, 'There he is!' do not believe it. For false messiahs and false prophets will appear and perform great signs and wonders to deceive, if

possible, even the elect. See, I have told you ahead of time. So if anyone tells you, 'There he is, out in the wilderness,' do not go out; or, 'Here he is, in the inner rooms,' do not believe it. For as lightning that comes from the east is visible even in the west, so will be the coming of the Son of Man (Matthew 24:4,5,11, 23-27 NIV).

The Apostle John said.

Many deceivers, who do not acknowledge Jesus Christ as coming in the flesh, have gone out into the world. Any such person is the deceiver and the antichrist (2 John 7 NIV).

According to John, there are already many "antichrists" in the world.

FALSE MESSIAHS HAVE COME AND WILL COME

Throughout the history of the church there have been those who have claimed to be the Christ and have gathered disciples. These false Christs fit the Scripture that tells us many antichrists shall come. Furthermore, false Christs will continue to appear until the Lord comes again.

THE FINAL ANTICHRIST

Although many antichrists will arise during the church age, the Bible speaks of a final Antichrist. He will come on the scene shortly before the Second Coming of Jesus Christ, the genuine Messiah. The name of this final Antichrist is taken from a statement made by John.

Dear children, this is the last hour; and as you have heard that the antichrist is coming, even now many antichrists have come. This is how we know it is the last hour (1 John 2:18 NIV).

Note that John speaks of "the" Antichrist who is coming.

THE RISE OF THE FINAL ANTICHRIST

This final Antichrist will rise to power, not as a religious leader, but as a political leader. He will head up a ten nation political confederation that will be a revival of the old Roman Empire. He will produce unity among this group while establishing himself as a strong political ruler. As the head of this confederation, he makes a covenant with the nation Israel, which gives the world the impression that he is a man of peace. Yet he will be the embodiment of evil.

THERE WILL BE A FALSE PEACE

The Bible says that one of the things that will characterize the environment in the "last days" is a false peace. Paul wrote about this to the Thessalonians.

> While people are saying, "Peace and safety," destruction will come on them suddenly, as labor pains on a pregnant woman, and they will not escape (1 Thessalonians 5:3 NIV).

Though this final Antichrist appears to be a man of peace, he is actually a man of deceit, energized by Satan. He will lead astray the people of the earth. What Alexander the Great purposed, world domination, he will take up and fulfill.

THE FINAL SEVEN YEARS

The coming Antichrist will have a period of seven years to do his evil work. This seven-year period is divided into two periods of three and one half years each. The first three and one half years will be a time of relative peace, where the people will be lulled by the Antichrist into the false notion that they are dwelling in safety.

HE WILL DEFILE THE TEMPLE

In the midst of the seven year-period, the final Antichrist will break his promises to the Jews, and begin persecuting them, as well as those who have believed in Jesus during the first half of this seven-year period.

It is during this three and one half year period that the great tribulation begins. The prophet Jeremiah spoke of this period as "the time of Jacob's trouble" (Jeremiah 30:7).

When the Antichrist breaks the covenant made with the Jews, he will "cause the sacrifice to cease." We read about this in the Book of Daniel.

> He will confirm a covenant with many for one week. But in the middle of that week he will bring sacrifices and offerings to a halt (Daniel 9:27 NET).

THE ABOMINATION OF DESOLATION IS *THE* KEY EVENT

As we have noted, this act of defiling the Temple is called, "the abomination of desolation." Jesus stated that this act would be the key event at the time of the end. We read.

> So when you see standing in the holy place 'the abomination that causes desolation,' spoken of through the prophet Daniel—let the reader understand. . . For then there will be great distress, unequaled from the beginning of the world until now—and never to be equaled again (Matthew 24:15, 21 NIV).

Jesus said this abomination will happen in the "holy place." The disciples would have understood this to be a reference to the Temple, as 19th century Bible commentator B.W. Newton notes.

> The expression "holy place" also, was one with which they were familiar. The well knew that there was but one spot in the whole of the earth of which that name would be used, viz., the Temple of Jerusalem. Jerusalem might be the Holy City, but the Temple was the Holy Place in the Holy City. Even then, if there had been nothing else to guide them, the well-understood meaning of the words, "abomination," "Holy Place," etc., would sufficiently have taught the

disciples to expect, not the overthrow of the Holy place, but the establishment of an Idol therein.[2]

There is something else the disciples would also have known; the historical precedent of this coming "abomination of desolation." It was a desecration in 167 B.C. by a ruler named Antiochus IV. There are a number of things we learn about the future abomination from what he did.

THE DESECRATION OF ANTIOCHUS: A TYPE OF THE FINAL ANTICHRIST

The defilement of the Second Temple, by Antiochus Epiphanes in 167 B.C., involved the stopping of the sacrifices, the enforcement of false worship, and the desecration of the Holy of Holies. It is a picture of what is to come. We can make the following comparisons.

To begin with, Antiochus, like the coming Antichrist, was a persecutor of the Jews. In particular, the Jews were set apart for horrific persecution by this evil ruler. Scripture says the final Antichrist will try to eliminate the entire Jewish race. However, like Antiochus, he will fail.

Antiochus was also involved in the defiling of the Holy Temple in Jerusalem. He placed idols in the Holy of Holies and slaughtered a pig on the altar of sacrifice. A similar thing will happen in the future. An image of Antichrist himself will be set up in a future Temple in Jerusalem. As we have emphasized, Jesus called this future incident "the abomination of desolation."

Antiochus, a political leader, worked with a religious leader. Antichrist will also have a religious leader promoting him. He is called the "second beast," or the "false prophet." This personage will force the people of the world to follow this man of sin, this Antichrist.

---

2. B.W. Newton, *The Prophecy Of Jesus as Contained in Matthew XXIV. & XXV. Considered*, London, Houlston and Sons, 1879, p. 54

Antiochus demanded worship. Like Antiochus of old, Antichrist will demand that everyone worship him as well as worship the devil. Those who do not will be put to death.

Antiochus was thought to be dead but appeared alive again. Antichrist will seemingly die or perhaps actually will die and then come back to life. His counterfeit resurrection will cause everyone in the world to marvel after him. It is at this time he demands the worship of the people.

There was a remnant of godly Jews who resisted Antiochus. In the same way, there will be a remnant of Jews who refuse to worship the beast. These Jews will be persecuted.

Finally, Antiochus was overthrown by a Jewish deliverer. The final Antichrist will be also be overthrown by a physical descendent of Abraham; the God/Man Jesus Christ.

Consequently, we find that Antiochus IV is the clearest pre-figurement or type that we have of the final Antichrist which is to come.

THERE IS NO DOUBT AS TO HOW THE DISCIPLES WOULD HAVE UNDERSTOOD JESUS' WORDS

B.W. Newton offers a fitting summary of how the disciples would have understood Jesus' words in light of what took place in 167 B.C. with Antiochus IV.

> The disciples were not only familiar with the meaning of the word "abomination" or "idol," as expressions; they were familiar also with a terrible and comparatively recent fact in the history of their nation—a fact that was still living in the remembrance of Israel. About 160 years previous to the Advent of the Lord, the most terrible persecutor whom the Jews had ever yet known—Antiochus Epiphanes—appeared in Jerusalem. He dedicated the temple to Jupiter Olympius,

and caused his image to be erected over the altar of burnt offering. The idol was set up in the Temple . . . [and] they began to offer sacrifices to this Idol. This profanation of the Temple of God had been prophetically foretold in the Scripture . . . Dan. Xi. 31. In the uninspired but authentic history of the first Book of the Maccabees it is referred to thus: "And on the fifteenth day of Casleu, in the hundred and forty-fifth year they set up the abomination of desolation . . . over the altar" [1 Maccabees 1:54]. The disciples were familiar with these passages in Daniel and in the Maccabees, as well as with the event described in them. When therefore the Lord Jesus again used the well-known expression "abomination of desolation," what could they expect but that a time should again come when an Idol should again be established and worshipped in the Temple of Israel. And so it will be.[3]

And so it will be indeed!

THE MAN OF SIN WILL TEMPORARILY SUCCEED

What Antiochus failed to achieve, this man of sin will attain. He will force Israel, and the entire world, to worship him. Those who do not will be put to death.

As we have already noted, the Apostle Paul tells us that this man will enter the Temple, and claim to be God.

> Don't let anyone deceive you in any way, for that day will not come until the rebellion occurs and the man of lawlessness is revealed, the man doomed to destruction. He will oppose and will exalt himself over everything that is called God or is worshiped, so that he sets himself up in God's temple, proclaiming himself to be God (2 Thessalonians 2:3,4 NIV).

This person "exalts himself above all that is called God."

3. B.W. Newton, *The Prophecy Of Jesus as Contained in Matthew XXIV. & XXV. Considered*, London, Houlston and Sons, 1879, pp. 54,55

WILL THERE BE A COUNTERFEIT RESURRECTION?

We mentioned that the final Antichrist may possibly pull off a counterfeit resurrection in his diabolical plan to divert the people from the true Messiah. First, we are told that he will seemingly have a mortal head wound.

> One of the heads of the beast seemed to have had a fatal wound, but the fatal wound had been healed. The whole world was filled with wonder and followed the beast. People worshiped the dragon because he had given authority to the beast, and they also worshiped the beast and asked, "Who is like the beast? Who can make war against it?" (Revelation 13:3-4 NIV).

We are also told of an image of this beast which is constructed for the purpose of worship. This image will be built by his cohort, the false prophet, also known as the "second beast." The Bible explains it this way.

> And, by the signs he [the false prophet] was permitted to perform on behalf of the beast, he deceived those who live on the earth. He told those who live on the earth to make an image to the beast who had been wounded by the sword, but still lived. The second beast was empowered to give life to the image of the first beast so that it could speak, and could cause all those who did not worship the image of the beast to be killed (Revelation 13:14-15 NET).

It is possible that the image is constructed to commemorate his "resurrection" from this mortal wound. The fact that the man of sin has had a resurrection-like experience is hinted at in Revelation 13:3,12. It is speculated that the final Antichrist is killed in battle and then returns to life to become a world dictator.

In addition, we find that those who refuse to worship the image of this beast will be put to death.

THE TIME OF THE GREAT TRIBULATION

The final Antichrist will then turn on both the Jews and the believers in Jesus, persecuting them and speaking blasphemies against God.

> So the beast opened his mouth to blaspheme against God-to blaspheme both his name and his dwelling place, that is, those who dwell in heaven. The beast was permitted to go to war against the saints and conquer them. He was given ruling authority over every tribe, people, language, and nation (Revelation 13:6,7 NET).

This will begin the time of the great tribulation. Jesus said of this period.

> For then there will be great distress, unequaled from the beginning of the world until now—and never to be equaled again (Matthew 24:21 NIV).

The reference to the time of "great tribulation" or "unprecedented trouble" goes back to a phrase in the book of Daniel. We read.

> At that time Michael, the great prince who protects your people, will arise. There will be a time of distress such as has not happened from the beginning of nations until then. But at that time your people—everyone whose name is found written in the book—will be delivered (Daniel 12:1 NIV).

Jesus said that the terrible judgments would be cut short for the sake of the survival of humanity.

> If those days had not been cut short, no one would survive, but for the sake of the elect those days will be shortened (Matthew 24:22 NIV).

For a limited period of time, this final Antichrist will be in control of everything.

SUMMATION OF THE CAREER OF THE FINAL ANTICHRIST

We can briefly sum up the career of this "man of sin" as follows.

1. The final Antichrist is last Gentile world ruler.

2. His identity will be revealed when he makes a seven-year covenant with the Jews.

3. He will arrive on the scene when the Temple at Jerusalem has been rebuilt and the Temple services are restored. In fact, he may be the one who allows the Temple to be rebuilt and the sacrifices reinstituted.

4. He will only be revealed when God begins to deal with the Jews nationally in their land.

5. He will suddenly stop the Temple sacrifices. He will defile the Temple when an image of himself is placed in the Holy of Holies.

6. This man will claim to be God. His cohort, the false prophet, will force the people of earth to worship this Antichrist and his image. Those who do not will be put to death.

This is how the Bible describes his career. It is clear that this final Antichrist has yet to appear (for more information on this personage see our book *The Final Antichrist: The Coming Caesar*).

THE THIRD TEMPLE WILL NOT EXIST FOR VERY LONG

The revival of the Temple sacrifices and services will be short-lived. What the final Antichrist permitted to be started, he will suddenly stop. He will do it for the same reason that Antiochus stopped the sacrifices in his day—to force the Jews to worship him.

However, his reign will also be short-lived. In fact, the Lord has told us that this final Antichrist will rule for only a limited period of time.

We will now consider what will take place when the reign of this man of sin comes to an end—the Second Coming of Jesus Christ!

SUMMARY TO CHAPTER 20

The Bible talks about the coming man of sin who makes a covenant with the Jews. The center stage for his actions will be the Third Temple. In the rebuilt Temple, this man declares himself to be God, and demands that the world worships him. This will mark the beginning of a period of time called by Jesus "the great tribulation"—a time of trouble that the world hasn't seen before or since.

This Antichrist will try to do what Haman, Hitler, and others have failed to accomplish—to destroy the race of Abraham. If Abraham's descendants would be obliterated, then the promises of God would be made void.

As this world ruler begins his "final solution" of the Jews the Bible says that they will turn to the One whom they rejected so long ago. It is only He who can deliver them from this horrible hour of trouble.

CHAPTER 21

Jesus Christ Returns: The End of the Third Temple and the Beginning of Peace on Earth

Look, he is coming with the clouds, and every eye will see him, even those who pierced him; and all peoples on earth will mourn because of him. So shall it be! Amen

Revelation 1:7

The history of Abraham's descendants testifies to the miraculous intervention, and providence, of God. Indeed, we find the beginning of his people starting with the supernatural birth of Isaac. Later, God intervened on Mt. Moriah and stopped Abraham from sacrificing his son of promise.

After the Exodus, God miraculously delivered the nation from Pharaoh's army at the Red Sea. During the time of Esther, God stopped Haman from destroying the entire nation. At the destruction of Jerusalem in A.D. 70, countless Jews lost their lives to the Roman army.

The unspeakable Holocaust of World War II cost the lives of one third of all the Jews living on the planet. Yet the Jews were not annihilated. Three years after the end of the Second World War, the modern state of Israel was formed.

THE WORST PREDICAMENT EVER FOR THE NATION

However, here at the end of this period of great tribulation, we find the Jews in their worst predicament ever. The person, who helped them rebuild their Temple, and reinstitute their sacrifices, is the one who turns on them, and attempts to destroy the entire nation. It is at this time, when they are seemingly without hope, that they will look for deliverance upon Him—the One whom they have pierced.

THE FINAL ANTICHRIST IS STOPPED

Antichrist's plan to rule the world, and destroy God's people, the Jews, is stopped by the Second Coming of Jesus Christ. The Bible says.

> Then I saw the beast and the kings of the earth and their armies gathered together to make war against the rider on the horse and his army. But the beast was captured, and with him the false prophet who had performed the signs on his behalf. With these signs he had deluded those who had received the mark of the beast and worshiped his image. The two of them were thrown alive into the fiery lake of burning sulfur. The rest were killed with the sword coming out of the mouth of the rider on the horse, and all the birds gorged themselves on their flesh (Revelation 19:19-21 NIV).

We also read in the Book of Revelation about the fate of the final Antichrist and his false prophet.

> And the devil, who deceived them, was thrown into the lake of burning sulfur, where the beast and the false prophet had been thrown. They will be tormented day and night for ever and ever (Revelation 20:10 NIV).

JESUS ENTERED JERUSALEM AS MESSIAH FROM THE MOUNT OF OLIVES

When the Lord Jesus entered Jerusalem at His triumphal entry, He came from the Mount of Olives. Matthew records that He fulfilled a prophecy made by Zechariah.

> Rejoice greatly, daughter of Zion! Shout, daughter of Jerusalem! Look! Your king is coming to you: he is legitimate

and victorious, humble and riding on a donkey on a young donkey, the foal of a female donkey (Zechariah 9:9 NET).

Zechariah has made another prophecy concerning the Mount of Olives—one that has yet to be fulfilled. He wrote the following.

On that day his feet will stand on the Mount of Olives which lies to the east of Jerusalem, and the Mount of Olives will be split in half from east to west, leaving a great valley. Half the mountain will move northward and the other half southward (Zechariah 14:4 NET).

JESUS WILL RETURN TO THE MOUNT OF OLIVES

When the Lord Jesus returns He will set His feet upon the Mount of Olives. The Bible records what happened at Jesus' ascension into heaven.

They [His disciples] were looking intently up into the sky as he was going, when suddenly two men dressed in white stood beside them. "Men of Galilee," they said, "why do you stand here looking into the sky? This same Jesus, who has been taken from you into heaven, will come back in the same way you have seen him go into heaven." Then the apostles returned to Jerusalem from the hill called the Mount of Olives, a Sabbath day's walk from the city (Acts 1:10-12 NIV).

The place where Jesus left this world, the Mount of Olives, is the place where He will return.

THERE WILL BE A CHANGED GEOGRAPHY

When Christ returns, the geography will be changed. Scripture says.

On that day living water will flow out from Jerusalem, half of it east to the Dead Sea and half of it west to the Mediterranean Sea, in summer and in winter (Zechariah 14:8 NIV).

The Lord will then set up His Kingdom, a kingdom of which there will be no end. Jesus will take His rightful place to the throne of David.

This eternal throne was promised to Him at the announcement to Mary of His coming birth. The angel Gabriel said to her.

> He will be great and will be called the Son of the Most High. The Lord God will give him the throne of his father David and he will reign over Jacob's descendants forever; his kingdom will never end (Luke 1:32,33 NIV).

The biblical prophecies concerning the Messiah will be fulfilled.

THE SECOND COMING OF JESUS CHRIST

As noted, the First Coming of Jesus did not mark His final appearance to planet earth. He is coming again! From the New Testament we can be assured of the following.

1. JESUS WILL PERSONALLY COME AGAIN

Jesus left no doubt that He would come back again. He said.

> My Father's house has many rooms; if that were not so, would I have told you that I am going there to prepare a place for you? And if I go and prepare a place for you, I will come back and take you to be with me that you also may be where I am (John 14:2,3 NIV).

The New Testament records many promises of His Second Coming. Indeed, the hope of believers, since Jesus Christ left earth and ascended into heaven, is that He will someday come again.

2. THERE IS NO END OF EVIL UNTIL HE RETURNS

Evil will continue to reign until His return. Jesus made this clear. He said.

You will hear of wars and rumors of wars, but see to it that
you are not alarmed. Such things must happen, but the end
is still to come. Nation will rise against nation, and kingdom
against kingdom. There will be famines and earthquakes in
various places (Matthew 24:6,7 NIV).

There will be no end to sickness, poverty, or crime until He returns.
While Christians should do everything they can to slow down evil, the
Bible says that evil will not be entirely done away with until Christ
returns a second time.

3. EVERYONE WILL SEE HIS RETURN

Although many false Christ's will arise before He returns, there will be
no doubt as to who the genuine Christ is. Jesus said.

For as lightning that comes from the east is visible even in
the west, so will be the coming of the Son of Man (Matthew
24:27 NIV).

We read in the Book of Revelation that every eye will see His coming.

Look! He comes with the clouds of heaven. And everyone will see him—even those who pierced him. And all
the nations of the world will mourn for him. Yes! Amen!
(Revelation 1:7 NIV).

Because Jesus told us the nature of His Second Coming, we can confi-
dently say that it has not yet occurred. When He does return, all of the
world will know.

4. THE ENTIRE WORLD WILL BE JUDGED

At His Second Coming, Christ will judge the nations. After He accom-
plishes this, He will set up His earthly kingdom. The Lord said.

When the Son of Man comes in His glory, and all the angels
with Him, then He will sit on the throne of His glory.

All the nations will be gathered before Him, and He will separate them one from another, just as a shepherd separates the sheep from the goats. He will put the sheep on His right and the goats on the left. Then the King will say to those on His right, 'Come, you who are blessed by My Father, inherit the kingdom prepared for you from the foundation of the world' (Matthew 25:31-34 HCSB).

THE DIVIDING OF THE SAVED AND THE LOST

The dividing of the sheep and the goats is the dividing of the saved and the lost. Those who have believed in Christ are saved from their sins and will enter into His kingdom. Those who have not believed will be punished for their unbelief and will not be allowed to enter into His glorious kingdom. Once this judgment is concluded the kingdom rule of the Lord Jesus will begin.

These events are yet to take place, but they are as certain to occur as those predictions by Jesus that have already been fulfilled.

5. THERE WILL BE GENUINE PEACE ON EARTH

When Jesus returns, the earth will experience the genuine peace it has been longing for since humankind first sinned against God. The Bible says.

In the last days the mountain of the LORD's temple will be established as the highest of the mountains; it will be exalted above the hills, and all nations will stream to it. Many peoples will come and say, "Come, let us go up to the mountain of the LORD, to the house of the God of Jacob. He will teach us his ways, so that we may walk in his paths." The law will go out from Zion, the word of the LORD from Jerusalem. He will judge between the nations and will settle disputes for many peoples. They will beat their swords into plowshares and their spears into pruning hooks. Nation will not take up sword against nation, nor will they train for war anymore (Isaiah 2:2-4 NIV).

The long-awaited predictions about peace on earth will be fulfilled with the Messiah ruling from His Temple—one built to honor Him. The Second Coming of Christ is the culmination of God's program for this planet.

JESUS' TEMPLE

When Jesus returns another Temple will be built. This Temple is described in Ezekiel 40-48. The millennial Temple that Ezekiel speaks of must not be confused with the tribulation Temple which is built in unbelief of Jesus. The millennial Temple is the Messiah's Temple—built to honor Him and Him alone. The sacrifices performed in this Temple will look back upon what God has done for humankind.

THE FATE OF THE TRIBULATION TEMPLE

What will become of this tribulation Temple? It will probably be destroyed sometime during the great tribulation, possibly during a huge earthquake. The Book of Revelation says.

> At that very hour there was a severe earthquake and a tenth of the city collapsed. Seven thousand people were killed in the earthquake, and the survivors were terrified and gave glory to the God of heaven (Revelation 11:13 NIV).

Such is the future fate of the people of Israel and the Third Temple.

THERE WILL BE NO TEMPLE IN ETERNITY

In the eternal realm, there will be no need for a Temple. The Bible tells us the following.

> I did not see a temple in the city, because the Lord God Almighty and the Lamb are its temple. The city does not

need the sun or the moon to shine on it, for the glory of God gives it light, and the Lamb is its lamp. The nations will walk by its light, and the kings of the earth will bring their splendor into it. On no day will its gates ever be shut, for there will be no night there. The glory and honor of the nations will be brought into it. Nothing impure will ever enter it, nor will anyone who does what is shameful or deceitful, but only those whose names are written in the Lamb's book of life (Revelation 21:22-27 NIV).

This is the glorious future for those who have placed their faith in Jesus Christ!

SUMMARY TO CHAPTER 21

According to the New Testament, after the Third Temple is built, it will be defiled and an image of this future world leader will be set up in the Holy of Holies. This one single act will begin a period of unprecedented judgments upon the earth called the great tribulation. This three and one half year period will culminate in the Second Coming of Christ to the earth.

The coming of Jesus Christ will put an end to this terrible time. He will return to earth, and then set us His eternal kingdom. The Lord will eventually create a new heaven and a new earth, where there will be no further need for a Temple. The Lord God Himself has promised that He will dwell with His people for all eternity. What a wonderful promise this is!

CHAPTER 22

Summing it All Up

But you, brothers and sisters, are not in darkness so that this day should surprise you like a thief. You are all children of the light and children of the day. We do not belong to the night or to the darkness. So then, let us not be like others, who are asleep, but let us be awake and sober

1 Thessalonians 5:4-6

As we sum up our study of the Jews, Jerusalem, and the coming Temple, there are certain matters with which we need to take special note. Indeed, the Temple Mount has been, and will continue to be, the scene of events that have tremendous Biblical significance.

THE TEMPLE MOUNT PAST

The Temple Mount past has been the center stage of important biblical events. The binding of Isaac by Abraham took place on Mt. Moriah, the mountain range in which Jerusalem was built upon. God led Abraham to a specific spot to build the altar to sacrifice Isaac.

Eventually David built an altar on the Temple Mount which would later become the site of the First Temple. Because of the sin of the people, the First Temple was destroyed. A Second Temple was built, and to it the Messiah came. Because Jesus was rejected, He predicted judgment upon the Second Temple. The Second Temple was destroyed, as Jesus had predicted, and the Jews were sent wandering for two thousand years.

THE PRESENT SITUATION

In 1948, the modern state of Israel was reborn. In 1967, the Israelis solidified Jerusalem. The present situation finds the control of Jerusalem with the Israelis, but the administration of the Temple Mount in the hands of Muslims—the same way it has been for the past eight hundred years. Preparations are now being made by certain Jews to build the next Temple, but the presence of two of the holiest buildings for Muslims—the Dome of the Rock Shrine and the Al Aqsa Mosque—stand in the way of any construction.

THE TEMPLE MOUNT IN THE FUTURE

The Temple Mount, which has figured so prominently in the plan of God for the past 4,000 years, has an inglorious future. According to Scripture, the Temple Mount will be center stage in important events in God's program. A seven-year covenant will be made between the coming world ruler (the final Antichrist), and the nation Israel. This peace agreement will probably allow Israel to rebuild their Temple and reinstitute their sacrifices. Therefore, a Third Temple will be built in unbelief of Jesus as the Messiah.

THE GREAT TRIBULATION

This next Temple will be the scene of the event that triggers the beginning of the great tribulation upon the earth. After a time of pseudo-peace, the man of sin breaks his covenant with the Jews and attempts to annihilate their race. An image of himself is placed in the Holy of Holies in the Temple and he declares himself to be God. The cohort of the final Antichrist, the false prophet, then forces the entire world to worship him.

THE SECOND COMING OF JESUS CHRIST

The career of the final Antichrist will end with the Second Coming of Christ to the earth. He will destroy the Antichrist, and false prophet, and then set up His kingdom upon the earth. The promise that Jesus gave when He left the first time—that He will return—will finally be fulfilled.

THE MILLENNIUM

When Christ returns, He will reign on the earth for one thousand years. This time is known as the Millennium. It will be characterized as a time of peace. During this millennial period there will be a new Temple in Jerusalem where all the nations will come and worship.

After the thousand years, God will create a new heaven and a new earth. Those who have believed God's promises will live forever with Him.

ISRAEL'S FOUR TEMPLES

When all is said and done, the nation Israel will have had four Temples in its history. They include the following.

1. The First Temple was Solomon's. It was built in 967 B.C. and destroyed in 587 B.C. by the Babylonians.

2. The Second Temple was that of Zerubbabel, a smaller version of Solomon's Temple. It was built after the destruction of the First Temple, and then later enlarged by King Herod. This is the Temple to which Jesus came. He predicted its destruction, and, as predicted, it was destroyed in the year A.D. 70.

3. The Third Temple is yet to be built. It will be built in unbelief of Jesus. Most likely it will be destroyed some time before He comes again.

4. The Fourth Temple is the Millennial Temple—the Temple of the Messiah Jesus. It will be built to honor Him.

UNRESOLVED MATTERS

There are still a number of important matters that remain unresolved with respect to the events surrounding the next Temple. These major issues are as follows.

1. Where To Build The Next Temple

2. How To Build On The Temple Mount

3. The Possible Role Of The Ark Of The Covenant

4. The Sacrifice Of The Red Heifer

5. How Soon A New Temple Can Be Built

6. The Involvement Of Christians In These Matters

All of these matters remain unresolved for the present time. We will look at the present situation of each of these.

UNRESOLVED PROBLEM 1: WHERE TO BUILD THE TEMPLE

There is the unresolved matter of where to build the next Temple. There are a number of possible sites.

1. The Dome of the Rock was the site of the Temple. The sacred rock was the location of the Holy of Holies.

2. The Dome of the Rock was the place of the Altar of Sacrifice. Thus the Temple stood slightly west of the Dome.

3. The Temple stood 330 feet to the north and the west of the Dome of the Rock.

4. The Temple stood somewhere south of the Dome of the Rock on the Temple Mount. It was located between the Dome and the Al Aqsa Mosque.

5. The Temple stood even further south of the Dome of the Rock near the Al Aqsa Mosque.

6. The Temple Mount of today is not where the original Temples stood. Instead they were located south of the Temple Mount in present-day Jerusalem.

There are experts who argue for each of these potential sites, except for the last one. Yet, no one knows for certain where the Temple exactly stood. Until work can be done on the Temple Mount itself, something impossible with the present political situation, the exact location of the Temple will remain a mystery.

UNRESOLVED PROBLEM 2: HOW TO BUILD THE TEMPLE

The greater problem is how to build the next Temple. With Islam in control of the Temple Mount, and not willing to give up even one inch of its territory, it seems an impossible matter for the next Temple to be built. Yet, we know from Scripture that a Third Temple will be constructed. Some type of political solution needs to come about to allow the Jews to build a Temple without causing the entire Muslim world to declare war on Israel.

The Bible predicts that a leader will come on the scene that seemingly has all the answers to the world's problems. It is most likely that this coming world ruler, the final Antichrist, will be the one who provides the solution on how to build the Third Temple without causing a "holy war" with Islam.

UNRESOLVED PROBLEM 3: THE ARK OF THE COVENANT

The Ark of the Covenant may play a part in the Third Temple. If discovered, it would certainly provide the momentum to build the next Temple. The Tabernacle, and then later the First Temple, were both constructed as a place to house the Ark. Though the Ark has been missing for 2,600 years, it is possible that it may still exist, and someday be found. We can only wait and see.

UNRESOLVED PROBLEM 4: THE ASHES OF THE RED HEIFER

Some insist that one of the requirements necessary for a Third Temple is the sprinkling of the ashes of the red heifer. As we have already noted, either the original ashes of the former red heifers will be found, or, more likely, a new red heifer will be sacrificed to purify the people. Randall Price aptly summarizes the situation.

> According to the rabbis of the Temple Movement, in order for a Temple to be rebuilt today, those who would enter the area of sanctity and perform the holy task must first be ritually pure. Since all Jews have become ceremonially unclean in the Diaspora, the only means to accomplish a reversal of this condition through the ashes of the Red Heifer (described in Numbers 19). Numerous attempts have been made, inside and outside Israel, to raise a qualified Red Heifer. Once this is accomplished it must be three years old before the ceremony of the Red Heifer can be conducted on the Mt. of Olives and the heifer burned and its ashes harvested for ritual purification.[1]

Therefore, it seems that some time before the next Temple is built, there will be the sprinkling of the ashes of a qualified red heifer.

UNRESOLVED PROBLEM 5: HOW SOON CAN THE TEMPLE BE BUILT?

Rabbi Chaim Richman, of the Temple Institute in Jerusalem, has stated publicly that a new Temple could be constructed within three to four months, once the go ahead is given. When a window of opportunity opens, it is surprising how quickly things can happen. It is only a matter of time as to when the next Temple will be built. So, it seems the Third Temple will be constructed very quickly once the roadblocks are cleared out of the way.

THERE IS NO PRECISE TIMETABLE

The Bible, however, does not give a precise timetable as to when the Temple will be built. Since the Bible does not specifically say, we can

---

1. Randall Price, *Rose Guide To The Temple*, Rose Publishing Inc., Torrance, California, 2012

only speculate. The only thing for certain is that it does exist in the middle of the seven-year period, the great tribulation. It does not have to be built before that time. Therefore, it could be standing for years, months, or merely weeks before the time of the "Abomination of Desolation." We simply do not know how long it will have been standing before it is desecrated.

MODERN TECHNOLOGY AND THE THIRD TEMPLE

As we have seen with the latest promotions from the Temple Institute the planned Third Temple will have all the latest modern technology. This will make Jesus' prediction, given so long ago, a worldwide reality when He said.

> So when you see standing in the holy place 'the abomination that causes desolation (Matthew 24:15 NIV).

With the help of modern technology everyone on the face of the earth will be able to actually "see" this tragic event.

UNRESOLVED PROBLEM 6: THE ROLE OF CHRISTIANS AND THE FUTURE TEMPLE

Christians are confronted with some important questions as to their involvement with the rebuilding of the Temple. What should a Christian do and not do?

THIS IS NOT OUR CAUSE

Though we know from the Scripture that a Third Temple is predicted, and will indeed be built, Christians should not participate in its planning, promotion, or construction. This is *not* our cause.

Some have argued that there was Gentile participation in building the First Temple so the same should be true with the "Coming Temple." However, Gentile participation in the building of the First Temple does not serve as a precedent for Gentile participation today. Those involved in building the First Temple were not Gentile believers. Their involvement was not due to their devotion to the God of Israel—rather, their services were conscripted. Therefore, to assert modern day Gentiles should help with the rebuilding of the Temple finds no Biblical basis.

THE TEMPLE WILL BE BUILT IN UNBELIEF OF JESUS

There is something else to consider. While the New Testament teaches that a Third Temple will be built, it also declares it will be built in unbelief of Jesus as the Messiah. The Third Temple will be ground zero for the activities of the man of sin, the final Antichrist. The future events surrounding the Third Temple will not honor Jesus in any way.

THERE IS NO FURTHER NEED FOR A TEMPLE

For the Christian there is no more need for a physical Temple. Jesus said about Himself, "something greater than the Temple is here" (Matthew 12:6).

When Christ died for the sins of the world He made direct access to God the Father possible. The Bible says.

> For there is one God and one intermediary between God and humanity, Christ Jesus, himself human (1 Timothy 2:5 NET).

The need for a Temple, and the sacrificial system, is now gone. Indeed, all of these things were fulfilled in the Person of Jesus Christ by His death on the cross and His resurrection from the dead. No more sacrifices are necessary! Those Christians who participate in the rebuilding efforts of the Third Temple would be sharing in the unbelief of the Jews.

WE CANNOT HASTEN THE COMING OF THE LORD TO THE EARTH

The motive of some, "to hasten the coming of the Lord," is equally a wrong motive. For one thing, God is running this universe according to His schedule, not ours. Furthermore, those Christians who want the

Temple built should realize that this will lead Israel into their worst Holocaust ever. There is no moral or Biblical justification in becoming involved in the building of the Third Temple. It is a Jewish cause.

ONE FINAL SUMMARY

The Bible has proven itself to be a reliable guide for the history of our planet. Much of God's program has, is, and will revolve around the Jews, the Holy City of Jerusalem, and the coming Temple.

As we mentioned in our introduction, God's prophetic clock, or time-piece, for the world is Israel. The nation Israel is compared to the "hour hand" on the clock while Jerusalem is the "minute hand" and the Temple Mount is the "second hand."

Consequently, while watching the world's headlines, we should keep our eyes on the Temple Mount for this one piece of real estate will find itself center stage for many prophetic events that will someday occur on the earth.

APPENDIX 1

A Scientific Search for
The Temple's Location (1983)

Though the original Temple was constructed some three thousand years ago it is possible that modern science, apart from on site archaeology, may be able to solve the mystery of where it once stood. Despite the research of Asher Kaufman, Leen Ritmeyer, Tuvia Sagiv and others, the exact spot where the First and Second Temples is still uncertain.

This uncertainty is what generated the interest of the author of this book to become involved in the quest for the actual Temple site. In 1982, he was put in contact with Lambert Dolphin, then Senior Research Physicist of the Science and Archaeology Laboratory of SRI International in Menlo Park, California.

At that time, SRI scientists had developed sophisticated geophysical equipment that helped "see into the ground." A brochure issued by SRI stated.

> Archaeology—the recovery, restoration, and preservation of priceless artifacts from the past—is a classic science requiring years of training, experience, patience, and arduous adherence to time honored disciplines. In recent years SRI scientists with equipment capable of "seeing through" rock—cultural scientists trained in electronic sensing, geophysical methods, and remote sensing—have begun successfully to apply these recent technologies to expedite the important work of the

archaeologist, anthropologist and historian. Remote sensing now offers an opportunity—for the first time—to explore and unearth some of man's great "lost" historic sites. Egypt and Israel offer particularly important opportunities.

The SRI equipment included a wall radar, seismic sounder, and cart mounted radar. If properly applied, this sophisticated equipment could, most likely, help solve the mystery of the location of the Temple.

THE EXPEDITION IS PLANNED

On a previous trip to Israel in 1982, the author spent considerable time with certain Israelis who were interested in determining the precise location of the Temple. He was invited to join an SRI expedition; if and when it ever came about. One of the Israelis had assured us that the Moslem Waqf would cooperate with what we were intending to do. We just had to keep a low profile.

THE GOODMAN INCIDENT

Plans were made to go to Israel in 1982 but were halted by the shooting on the Mount by Israeli soldier Allan Goodman. The trip was postponed to let tensions settle down. What appeared to be a good opportunity was now postponed and possibly cancelled.

ANOTHER TRIP PLANNED

After letting the tensions cease for a while another trip was planned in April/May of 1983. As we were about to leave we received the following Western Union Mailgram from Israel on April 8, 1983.

> Necessary authorities oppose project this time owing to adverse press. Regretfully must recommend postponement.
>
> Theo

Although this Israeli contact suggested we postpone again, we decided the trip should go ahead. In April-May of 1983 a seven-man team headed by Lambert Dolphin, and including the author of this book, made a six-week geophysical survey in Israel. The group made use of SRI's highly sophisticated equipment including cart radar, wall radar, seismic sounder, and high resolution resistivity. This non-destructive equipment was used on various archaeological sights in an attempt to determine what lay beneath the surface.

Our goal was to use the equipment as near as we could to the Temple Mount. However, before attempting that delicate task we decided to try out this sophisticated hardware on other sites. Working with several noted Israeli archaeologists we applied the equipment to a number of places around the country. Happily, the equipment worked very well causing one archaeologist to exclaim, "It works like magic." Assuredly there was no magic involved merely the careful skillful application of radar and sonar waves among the ancient ruins of Israel.

The instruments showed the archaeologists some very promising possibilities as to where to excavate.

THE RABBINICAL TUNNEL

Since 1967, an excavation sponsored by the Ministry of Religious Affairs has been going on near the prayer area of the Western Wall of the Temple Mount. In the beginning, the work had achieved little notoriety. The project consists of a tunnel running some 900 feet, running north alongside the Western Wall. The tunnel cuts its way beneath shops and houses in the Arab section of the Old City of Jerusalem. This site, hidden from public view, is known as the Rabbinical Tunnel.

In 1982, the tunnel was not accessible to the general public. On a trip to Israel in that year, the author, along with Pastor Chuck Smith of Calvary Chapel of Costa Mesa, California, had the unique privilege to explore this magnificent site. It was an unforgettable experience.

At that particular time, we had to enter from a locked metal door starting the journey some sixty feet above the bedrock at the hall under what is known as Wilson's Arch. However, as we walked this level tunnel, the bedrock was rising. When we reached the northern end of the tunnel we were about thirty feet *below* the bedrock's upper surface. The damp tunnel has a well lit corridor that is approximately seven feet high and five feet wide. We walked upon wooden floorboards.

There is one particularly amazing sight that stole our attention soon after we entered. It is a gigantic stone that is 46 feet long, over 10 feet high and about 10 feet thick. It is one solid piece of hewn limestone weighing over 600 tons! How the ancient builders brought that huge stone one half miles from the quarry is not known. It is also unknown how they were able to place the stones so precisely in the wall that a knife blade cannot slip in between the seams of the stones. This huge stone was one of many fascinating sights in the Rabbinical Tunnel.

A walk through the tunnel tends to put a person in a reflective mood when one thinks about the history that took place in and around these walls.

Since we could not operate with our equipment from the Temple Mount, the plan was that our work would have to be carried out from this tunnel.

A SCIENTIFIC EXPEDITION IS THWARTED

On May 22, 1983 our team of eight people, including our affable Jewish guide, Stanley Goldfoot, attempted to make the first scientific survey of the rabbinical tunnel. The object was to use our highly sophisticated equipment, including wall penetrating radar and seismic sounding, to look into the wall toward the Temple Mount in hopes of determining at least four things:

1) The thickness of the wall.

2) Any large open spaces inside the wall which could indicate a water cistern, a tunnel or a secret room.

3) The foundations of the Western Wall of the Second Temple or other structures. (The foundation stones may still be in place. Jesus predicted one stone would not be left upon another, but this may not include the foundation stone that is resting upon the bedrock).

4) Anything that had not been discovered thus far.

We went by night for two reasons. First we needed the quiet so that the instruments, especially the seismic sounder, could work at its best capacity, without interference of city noises and the workmen in the tunnel. Second, we thought it best to keep our mission quiet because the more people who knew about it the more complicated things became.

We arrived at the compound of the Western Wall at 10 p.m. The guard at the gate was about to let our van proceed when we were suddenly met by plain clothes detectives. They inquired as to what we were going to do. We told them who we were and that we had been invited by Rabbi Getz, the man in charge of the tunnel, to do some scientific work for him. After examining our passports, they called in their boss. After talking to us for a while he said that we could not come in because we did not have the proper permits. We were instructed to see a certain high official the next day who could grant us the proper permission. Thus we went back to the hotel, with a van full of unloaded equipment determined to get the proper permit first thing the next morning.

THE PEOPLE WERE AFRAID OF A RIOT

However, a meeting with the chief of police intelligence early the next morning revealed that we needed no permit whatsoever. We were duly informed that the government police knew everything about us, who we were, why we were coming, and that they were placed at the compound to stop us.

The reason for this was they had received a call from the Waqf (the Muslim authority over the Temple Mount) that went as follows: "some scientists from America are going to place electronic equipment underneath our Mosque, please stop them."

The chief detective said that we had done nothing wrong and that which we were trying to do was a legal and a worthy venture. However, they feared what the Muslims might do if we were allowed to continue. Therefore, to avoid a possible riot and international incident (as had occurred with the ill-fated Parker expedition), we were refused permission to enter. They were sympathetic to our effort, going out of their way to make sure we were not offended. They told us that it was their hope that we could, sometime soon, return and perform our desired task.

However, since the Muslims did not understand our equipment they most likely assumed it to be something destructive rather than constructive.

The conclusion of the whole episode can be summed up as follows: Even though the rabbinical tunnel is on Jewish property and we had a request by those who have charge of it to perform a legitimate scientific study, we could not do it because of Muslim objections. Thus, the Muslims seemingly have veto power over what goes on in the tunnel as well as upon the Temple Mount. The authorities, wanting to keep the status quo, bent to the Muslim wishes in hopes to avoid possible confrontation. Needless to say, the situation remains highly volatile.

Naturally we were disappointed that we could not perform the purpose of our trip to Israel. Though we were foiled in our attempt to use the equipment on or near the Temple Mount, we were confident that if we were given the chance again, the team could accomplish something significant. We knew that the equipment can and does work in the terrain of Israel.

EXPEDITION RECEIVES NOTORIETY

Though we did not achieve our desired goal our expedition did attract attention. The *Jerusalem Post* ran the following story.

Arming archeologists with electronic devices to probe the ground would seem to take the sporting element out of the exercise—like providing bullfighters with RPG's.

But Israeli archeologists, like their colleagues abroad, have been quick to place science above sport when offered the opportunity of abetting their instincts with electronics.

Some of the most sophisticated equipment in the world for taking soundings through the ground and thick walls was recently employed on several of the most notable digs in the country by an American group that developed its expertise in defence work for the U.S. government.

The group, headed by physicist Lambert Dolphin, is part of SRI International of Menlo Park, California. . . They brought with them equipment that included ground-penetrating radar and electrodes employed in a "high resolution automatic resistivity" method said to be capable of drawing an underground contour map. . .

In Hebron, the team took readings of the ground beneath the Tomb of the Patriarchs while remaining outside the structure. However, the planned highlight of the visit—a probe of the Temple Mount—did not come off.

Dolphin said he had received permission from the rabbi of the Western Wall, Rabbi Yehuda Getz, to position his equipment in the tunnel dug by the Religious Affairs Ministry north of the Western Wall. His intention was to probe electronically beneath the mount to see whether he could find indications of subterranean passages in which objects of historical or religious significance may have been buried.

However, as the team approached the tunnel they were intercepted and turned back by Israeli police operating at the behest of the Supreme Muslim Council, which had apparently been warned of their activities by Muslim officials in Hebron.

The trip also received publicity in the United States. *The Sacramento Bee* ran the following story:

IMAGINE INDIANA JONES WITH HAN SOLO GADGETRY

The tomb lay buried—secreted under a fall of rock from another burial site.

For centuries, grave robbers passed it by. Archeologists, armed with educated guesses, fumbled blindly around it.

It took British archeologist Howard Carter six years of searching through hot dust and rocks before in 1922, he uncovered the tomb of Tutankhamen, boy king of Egypt. It had stayed untouched, crammed with the trappings of a king, for more than 3,000 years.

Recently a group of California engineers retraced Carter's tracks. Standing as he did in a dark tomb above Tutankhamen's, they set up acoustic sound equipment.

It took them thirty minutes to get a reading on the burial site beneath their feet. "That's what we can do best-save time," says Lambert Dolphin, a physicist with SRI International, a private research firm in Menlo Park. Dolphin was one member of the team that "rediscovered" Tut's tomb. . .

As well as working in Egypt, the SRI team has helped sort through buried cities in Israel. Last year, it discovered a chamber inside what was thought to be a solid tower in the mountain fortress of Herodium, the summer residence of Herod the Great. Israeli archeologists excavating the site think the chamber—15 feet in diameter—could be the tomb of Herod, who ruled from 73 B.C. to 4 A.D. Archeologists have been searching for the tomb, thought to be full of gold and artwork for years.

"We've given some hot leads in a needle-in-a-haystack search" Dolphin said. But now they still have to do the excavation and that takes time. I want to make the point that archeology is a time-honored profession and while this equipment can help, it will never replace the plain old hard work.

Because the team had possibly discovered Herod's tomb, the wire services picked up the story and it became printed nation wide. Some of the headlines read as follows.

PHYSICIST SAYS HE HAS FOUND HEROD'S TOMB,

The New Haven Connecticut Register, October 30, 1983

GEOPHYSICIST LOOKS FOR HEROD'S TOMB WITH AID OF RADAR, SONAR

Times Union, Albany, N.Y., November 24, 1983

The SRI team *never* claimed to have found Herod's tomb, only a possible site. However, some of the newspapers did sensationalize the story making our expedition seemingly the discoverers of Herod's burial place.

Ehud Netzer, the excavator of Herodium, did not believe Herod was buried in the chamber in the tower which we discovered. In fact, Herod's tomb was later discovered in a different location.

However, what the expedition did prove was that the equipment works. The tower in which the chamber was discovered was always thought to be solid. No one would have ever bothered attempting to excavate it if it were not for the wall penetrating radar. The work at Herodium proved again what a valuable service these instruments can render. If applied to the Temple Mount the same results could be obtained.

MORE CONTROVERSY

An article that appeared in the *Jerusalem Post* further fueled the controversy. It read as follows.

> There are significant, and to some minds worrisome links between a handful of American Evangelical leaders and right-wing Israelis like [Stanley] Goldfoot. Some of the personalities on his board are important men. Lambert Dolphin, heads a key section of the world's most massive research conglomerate, the Stanford Research Institute, a $200-million-a-year concern whose main clients are the U.S. government and corporations like Bechtel . . .
>
> Before the Temple Mount plotters—both the Lifta terrorists and the Gush Emunim terror group—were arrested, Goldfoot and Dolphin planned to hover one day just before dawn in a helicopter 300 metres above the Temple Mount and the Holy of Holies (where the Ark of the Covenant was kept), and to X-ray and probe the innards of the mount with Dolphin's induced polarization set, Cesium Beam Magnatometer, downhole Borescope television and high-power Dipole-Dipole Resistivity Set to find out just what is buried down there . . . Along with Lambert Dolphin they [Other Christian Temple Mount Activists] condemned the abortive attempt (by the Lifta Group) to blow up the Dome of the Rock. But they feel "violence" is being done to the most sacred site "when Jewish prayer books are seized by Temple Guards from devout Jewish women.

Because of the numerous inaccuracies in the article Lambert Dolphin immediately sent a letter to the *Jerusalem Post*. It reads in part:

> Your article . . . contains so many distortions of fact and so much vilification directed at well intentioned Israelis and friends of friends of Israel I can not help but wonder if

this is part of a conspiracy of some kind? I deeply regret the cheap attacks on my good friend Stanley Goldfoot who has spent much time and taken much trouble to free me from anti-Semitism and ignorance of Jewish values and Jewish consciousness.

The latter trip [to Israel] when I was accompanied by six colleagues consisted of donated geophysical services to half a dozen leading Israeli archaeologists intended to advance the state of Archaeological knowledge and methodology in Israel. This work was paid for by four American Christians and one Jewish businessman. All funds were used for team expenses and salaries. No funds were donated or passed to any individual or group in Israel. I regret not having additional funds, as I would be glad to contribute them to your nation's leading archaeologists to be used at their discretion for their important excavation work.

I . . . am not a member of the Jerusalem Temple Foundation nor do I wish to participate in the building planning or program. This effort, I believe, is part of the Jewish religious economy, not the calling of God for the church. Of course I would like to see the Temple Mount explored scientifically and non-destructively apart from all religious and political considerations. I believe freedom of worship and prayer on the Temple Mount should now be extended to include Jews and Christians and that by faith the Jewish people should regain administration of the Temple Mount as part of your own legitimate religious and Biblical heritage given you by God. I deplore the widespread apathy, indifference and hostility toward the holy one in the holy land knowing this only speeds the "time of Jacob's trouble" which will be marked by terrible trial and much suffering as the prophets have all said. Israel's glorious destiny is sure and for that I rejoice.

You seem to not need any external enemies since there is so much in-country backbiting, character assassination and self-destructiveness. Friends you do need, and I remain a friend and supporter of the people and state of Israel in spite of being misunderstood and misrepresented.

As of today, no one knows for certain which of the possible sites on the Temple Mount was the place where the First and Second Temple stood. If our team had been permitted to use the sophisticated equipment in the Rabbinical Tunnel, then we have reason to believe that we may have been able to help solve the problem.

Unfortunately, we never had the chance to go back to the Temple Mount with the equipment. To this day, the exact location as to where the Temple stood remains unsolved.

About The Author

Don Stewart is a graduate of Biola University and Talbot Theological Seminary (with the highest honors).

Don is a best-selling and award-winning author having authored, or co-authored, over seventy books. This includes the best-selling *Answers to Tough Questions*, with Josh McDowell, as well as the award-winning book *Family Handbook of Christian Knowledge: The Bible*. His various writings have been translated into over thirty different languages and have sold over a million copies.

Don has traveled around the world proclaiming and defending the historic Christian faith. He has also taught both Hebrew and Greek at the undergraduate level and Greek at the graduate level.

57929758R00150

Made in the USA
Charleston, SC
26 June 2016